Get the Career You Want

Teach® Yourself

Get the Career You Want

Karen Mannering

Hodder Education

338 Euston Road, London NW1 3BH.

Hodder Education is an Hachette UK company

First published in UK 2011 by Hodder Education

First published in US 2011 by The McGraw-Hill Companies, Inc.

British Library Cataloguing in Publication Data: a catalogue record for this title is available from the British Library.

Library of Congress Catalog Card Number: on file.

10 9 8 7 6 5 4 3 2 1

Year 2015 2014 2013 2012 2011

The publisher has used its best endeavours to ensure that any website addresses referred to in this book are correct and active at the time of going to press. However, the publisher and the author have no responsibility for the websites and can make no guarantee that a site will remain live or that the content will remain relevant, decent or appropriate.

The publisher has made every effort to mark as such all words which it believes to be trademarks. The publisher should also like to make it clear that the presence of a word in the book, whether marked or unmarked, in no way affects its legal status as a trademark.

Every reasonable effort has been made by the publisher to trace the copyright holders of material in this book. Any errors or omissions should be notified in writing to the publisher, who will endeavour to rectify the situation for any reprints and future editions.

Hachette UK's policy is to use papers that are natural, renewable and recyclable products and made from wood grown in sustainable forests. The logging and manufacturing processes are expected to conform to the environmental regulations of the country of origin.

www.hoddereducation.co.uk

Typeset by MPS Limited, a Macmillan Company.

Printed in Great Britain by CPI Cox & Wyman, Reading.

Acknowledgements

I would like to thank Alison Frecknall, Elizabeth Pilcher and Georgia-Karena Mannering for their help with this book.

Contents

Meet the author

We all have moments when we feel that life becomes boring or tedious. A change of job or career can be therapeutic in giving us a new perspective on our working lives. However, not everyone can just up and change their job, and there are many reasons for this. Perhaps you are stuck in a job that seems to be going nowhere but there is no alternative employment in your area at the moment. Perhaps your specialism has become a limitation. Or maybe you feel suddenly constrained by the long-term job security that appealed to you so much in the first place. There are a myriad of reasons why anyone might feel suddenly uncomfortable in their job and long to break out.

In my career I have coached many people with their careers both from the perspective of helping them to apply their skills better to their current job, and also to find other employment opportunities. When leaving is on the agenda one factor is always very evident: in their need to move on very few people really recognize what they are leaving behind. All jobs have their good and bad aspects but when we feel cornered or want to move on, we fail to see the good things and exaggerate the bad. This means that we do not always have a balanced view of the situation. How many times have you heard someone say, 'I was desperate to move but I wish I had not bothered now'? Magazines are always telling you to 'move on' or 'move up' but that is not always the best approach for building a solid career. Constant job-hopping works in very few industries and even new job opportunities dry up eventually (leaving you with a CV that looks like you cannot settle anywhere).

Of course not everyone has the ability to move job. If you have enrolled in a long period of service or study, you cannot simply walk out without considering all the implications. Your career may be for life, but suddenly you find yourself wondering if this is the life you envisaged. Perhaps there is a downturn in your industry and opportunities are few.

While others are telling you how lucky you are, you might just feel trapped and lonely in a diminishing business area.

I believe that there are times when a new job is a breath of fresh air and just the right thing, but there are also times when it is important to sit fast and gain greater satisfaction from the job you are in. There may be many aspects to your job that you have not considered, aspects that can revitalize you and make you literally fall in love with your job all over again. Impossible? Not necessarily. After all, your job must have been desirable to you once. Like all good relationships, jobs mature as you learn more about them and the initial excitement wanes. Recapture that excitement and bingo! – suddenly you are looking forward to every new day once again.

Whether you decide to leave or stay, the important thing is that you make that decision based on solid thinking and sound knowledge. This sound basis is what I aim to provide in this book, so that you can make the choices that enable you to have a full and successful working life.

Karen Mannering, 2011

Only got a minute?

If you only have one minute, hold back and don't do anything rash. Don't walk out or say anything to anyone. Take three deep breaths and then try these two exercises. Firstly, on a piece of paper, write a list of positive words related to your job – no negatives allowed! While you are doing this, think about your colleagues, your manager, the work itself – imagine you are working for a promotions agency that needs to sell your company. Don't lie, but be positive. You may find yourself using words such as 'energizing', 'dynamic', 'friendly'. Look down the list and ask yourself if you met someone at a party and they used these words to describe their job, wouldn't you want to work for that company? No job is interesting every moment of every day, but it is how we choose to see the job and its attributes.

The second quick exercise is to find a quiet corner, close your eyes and remember why you took this job in the first place. Perhaps you had been trying to break into this field for some time or this was the hundredth application, or maybe it was because your friend or family worked there. Try to conjure up the feelings of excitement you had when you learned you had been accepted for the job. Has the job changed or is it you? Those feelings are not very far away and can easily be rekindled.

Introduction

There are many career books on the market but most of them are focused on the external aspects of career choice, such as how to perform in an interview or what to write in psychometric tests. I could not find a book that looked at who you are and led you to question what skills you have that you could utilize at work to create a fulfilling career that is the right fit for you. It is not enough to think of a career in terms of job title – you have to be aware of how the job fits your characteristics.

I also find that, in general, career books are very focused on moving the reader on from their current position and finding 'Nirvana' elsewhere. This is not always realistic. In the current financial climate I would suggest not storming out of one job because you feel the need to change, because quite simply there may not be another along immediately. There is also the situation that you just might find that the job you coveted is actually under your very nose. We are all as guilty of thinking that the grass is greener elsewhere as small girls who think that all life's problems can be solved by becoming a princess. A nice thought but not in step with reality. Quite often the 'devil we know' really is better than the one we don't!

Speaking of reality, I also believe it is never too late to explore a new career area, especially if you are willing to be flexible. For example, you may have left it a little late to play the flute as a career in a professional orchestra, but you can gain immense satisfaction from playing the same instrument in a local community orchestra.

In this book I am encouraging you, the reader, to explore your dissatisfaction with your current job and also to recognize where you have particular strengths to take forward into any future career. I am also suggesting that you should start by analysing your current job *before* moving on. Sometimes we all think that a change is needed when in fact it is a change in our thinking that brings the greatest results. If you are currently unemployed, use the activities in Part four to identify your skills and think about where your future career lies.

This book is in four parts. Part one asks you to consider the history of how you came to be in the job you are currently in. Part two looks at your current situation, while Part three moves you forward into the future. Throughout the book there are activities to complete – find them in Part four. Some of the activities are to help you gain a greater understanding of yourself, while others aim to help you think or act differently. All of the activities can be revisited again and again, and therefore you need never be without the tools and techniques you need for the remainder of your career – whatever direction you decide to take.

To help you put the activities into context, I have created five characters which appear at the end of Parts one, two and three in the form of case studies, so let's find out more about these characters and their situations.

CAROL

Carol is 47 and has worked at Morgan Pilchard for two years. Morgan Pilchard is an accountancy office, and Carol does basic administration work. She did not really want to work there specifically but it was a local job and they seemed quite nice. Carol married young and never had time to establish a career before starting a family. She had four children (all now grown up and living elsewhere) and in the intervening years, Carol worked in a couple of shops, mainly on the tills or filling shelves. Carol went on a re-skilling course when she was 45 and learned how to use computers and undertake basic office duties. She attained an NVQ in Administration and this was the first qualification she had ever held; consequently this gave her a lot of confidence. During her course she realized that she had never held a job with significant responsibility but now wants to try to stretch herself in the last of her working years. She is not sure whether she really wants to leave Morgan Pilchard or not, because she does not really know what she is capable of or what else could be available elsewhere.

SAMIA

Samia is 25 and left school with three A-levels. She did not want to go to university and so went straight into an apprenticeship in a factory, working on producing estimates for plastic mouldings. The factory is a major employer in the area and she initially felt glad that her grades allowed her to slide straight into an office job, rather than be on the factory floor, but she is starting to rethink that. She has recently found out that, even though the company has just won a very large contract, they are going to have a reorganization and that could result in fewer office staff in her particular unit in the future. Factory floor staff will remain unchanged. At the moment management are saying that there will not be redundancies for those who are prepared to be flexible, and move into other jobs, but Samia is worried because she has not been trained to do anything else. Samia was not given any career advice at school and is now starting to panic. She is having trouble thinking through her options, and feels she has nowhere to turn. All this is further complicated by the fact that Samia is trying to organize her wedding next year. Losing her job would be a disaster and probably mean that she would not secure the mortgage she wants and she would have to postpone the wedding.

JASON

Jason is 19 and has taken a job in the same factory as Samia. He drifted into this job from school as, at the time, he did not want to feel different from his friends, and he wanted to earn his own money. At first his job seemed easy and 'money for old rope' but now it is boring and it has suddenly hit him that this is the way his working life will be if he does not make some changes; another 40 years of doing the same thing. Jason is stunned by the realization that when he was at school all he wanted was to get out into the world, but now he is there he wonders what the rush was. He feels ready to go back to the drawing board and rethink his options before it is too late. He also would not relish giving up his pay.

HENRI

Henri is 51 and has recently been made redundant. It has come as a total shock to him because he thought he was in a secure job. Henri was a senior manager in local government and managed a large team of people responsible for regeneration projects. He knew the council had to make changes and he had put a number of ideas forward, but was stunned when the council cut out a management level, and that included him. Henri is married to Alice (a school teacher) and they have three children, the youngest is still at university. Henri is finding it difficult to reconcile his position because he had thought that he had a secure job for life. Also senior management and 'working your way up through the organization' used to be the guarantee of a stable future – not make you more vulnerable! It seems to Henri that all the rules have changed, and he is feeling very low about his situation. Nobody employs people over 51 these days, do they?

CHRIS

Chris is 35 and, until recently, worked in an estate agency. She has been there since she was 16 and although she had time off for maternity leave she has worked there ever since. When her children were very young she worked part-time and weekends, but then went back to full-time work, five years ago. She has found them to be a very flexible employer and she loved her work, getting great pleasure from finding the right house for many families. She used her instinct a lot in her work and she was very successful but a change of behaviour in the house-buying public has resulted in a drop in house stock to sell. This means that, without so many houses to sell, the agency needed fewer staff. Although the agency values Chris they have acted dramatically by deciding to lose all jobs that could not be covered by the partners plus one secretary. Chris has suddenly found herself without a job and there are no other openings in the estate agency business, because the problem is widespread in that industry. Chris knows that this is probably a temporary problem, that there are no guarantees for the long-term future and that she cannot afford to wait just in case things change. She needs to rethink her future and where she goes from here.

OK, let's get started!

Part one

Your journey so far

1

Taking stock of your career history

In this chapter you will learn:
- *to reflect on your career history*
- *to evaluate your current situation*
- *to analyse your career path*

Employment will take up a large part of your life. It is a sobering fact that you will spend more time at work with people you have not chosen to be with than with those you do choose to be with at home. It is for this reason that you must find a career that offers you some stimulation or enjoyment. Life is too short to waste it on working in a place or position you find unsatisfactory.

Your career: your life

Your career progression may also not always go completely to plan. People can find themselves in the wrong career and wishing they had chosen something else, or in the right career but at the wrong time, or even in the right career but bored through lack of opportunity.

For whatever reason, it is good to go back to basics and think through what a career is and how we came to be in the place we are at, before we begin to make plans for the future. If you are not happy in your career there are ways to prepare to make the change, but as the proverb says, 'every journey begins with a first step'. Make this your first step to creating a more fulfilling future from now on.

JOB VERSUS CAREER

We are all supposed to have career paths these days, but what actually is a career? In the past, careers were the preserve of professionals, and everyone else had a job. This was the typical 'blue' collar/'white' collar split, where you were in one group or the other. Blue-collar workers were the workforce and white-collar workers were typically management. That categorization in itself has caused polarization and entrenchment over the years. However, we use the term much more loosely these days and tend to ask everyone what they have chosen as a career.

Essentially a job is any form of work, while a career has a pathway that is well defined, possibly with promotional prospects, and is set within an industry that has a future. A career is more likely (although not always) to be vocational too.

A career path is perceived as a steady incremental march in one direction, to attain a certain level or goal. Jobs may come and go but your career path has a designed direction, for example, a career in banking. To take a job may involve little or no forethought but to start a career in any subject is to have taken a decision that this is the path in life that you choose to travel. Jobs can just happen along the way, but careers are usually planned.

Occasionally a career is not planned as such, but you can suddenly find yourself in one. Just suppose you followed your parents into a family business, or perhaps you took a job initially at a low level but then stayed on, progressing and developing, until suddenly you found yourself locked into a career. You may not have chosen this particular career path had you sat down and planned your own future, but it crept up on you incrementally, and it seemed easy to become engrossed. You went along with it but now you are stuck, frustrated or perhaps bored. What can you do about this? This book will provide you with a range of techniques to think through your career so that you are sure you are in the right place for you.

HOW OUR CAREER DEFINES US

When I finished school in the late 70s there was very little choice concerning your next move. If you were academic and achieved good grades you were pointed towards university; if you showed an interest and skill in more practical applications, you went to college, perhaps in conjunction with an apprenticeship. The rest of the school leavers went to work in whatever job they could find, perhaps in the local industry or the high street, or they joined the services. These choices were further complicated by our upbringing and family expectations, not to mention societal influences.

That then became our destiny. It was extremely rare for a mature person to go to university later on, or break away from their mould, and there was a feeling of our fate in life being set in concrete – after all, your job was not everything and you had other things in your life to think about. Most jobs were for life and we had a tendency to accept our fate.

As we got older, our job started to define us. When meeting for the first time, the second question that most people asked after the initial, 'What is your name?' was inevitably, 'And what do you do?' Like it or not, the answer you gave categorized how that person viewed you from thereon. Based on your answer they would decide:

▶ how much they feel they should listen to you (should they bother to give you 'air time'?)
▶ the extent to which your views will be affected by your job (ask a police officer about law and you might get a different view than that from any member of the public)
▶ whether they even want to listen to you (some jobs can make others feel uncomfortable or less relaxed, such as being a vicar)
▶ whether they feel you might be a good contact for the future (people in the media industry always seem popular)
▶ what personality type you might have (an artist may be perceived as free spirited and difficult to deal with while an accountant may be perceived as pedantic)
▶ how interesting and erudite you might be (people with an interesting job that they can convey in witty stories will be perceived to be more interesting than someone with a narrow background)
▶ how hard working you are (a nurse will possibly be perceived as working harder than a record producer).

Finally, a value of you as a person might also be ascribed (for example, it might be perceived that a doctor makes more of a contribution to society than a model or a pop star).

Already our choice of job or career is starting to define us, creating the circles within which we socialize and displaying our image to the world. But what if this is not the image we want to create? What if we don't feel comfortable in our present mould and really always wanted to be something else?

The good news is that things are very different today. School leavers have so much more choice and anyone can choose to return to learning at any stage of their life. Suddenly our lives are no longer preordained, and we can have many different careers in our own working lifetime. However, although the social situation has changed, human evolution has not had time to catch up, and the job you are doing will still define you and create an image both in your own eyes and those of others. For this reason it is important to feel comfortable with your choice. Is the image of your job the one you want to project? We are all our own advert and people will make assumptions (however unfair) about us based on that. Are you comfortable with your chosen career and what it says about you? Look at Activity 1 in Part four of this book to find out.

HOW MUCH GUIDANCE DID YOU HAVE?

Think back to when you were at school. How much guidance and help did you have on selecting a career? Career advice varies considerably and, in schools, career officers often have very little training. The good news is that there are now plenty of websites such as the government site www.nextstep.direct.gov.uk to help you. Also many Job Centres now offer a more sophisticated package for helping people decide what career would suit them best.

Career advisers are now able to use psychometrics (measurement questionnaires) to determine:

▶ your personality type – Some personality traits fare better in some careers, for example, people who are extrovert are better suited to sales than an introvert. This does not mean that introverts cannot become sales professionals; it just means that they may find it more of a challenge because the nature of the job is to be highly socially interactive.

- ▶ your preferences – Do you prefer detailed work or more broad-brush large concepts and 'blue-sky' thinking? I would certainly want my accountant to pay attention to the detail in my accounts and would not thank them for sitting back, thinking through the possibilities of future business. Similarly, I would expect a company director to be able to analyse the way in which the business is moving and be able to see the 'big picture' rather than worry about the performance of each individual member of staff. Knowing your preferences for the way in which you work can help you see that certain people flourish in jobs that contain the qualities they possess.
- ▶ the types of activity you most enjoy – Some people enjoy working in a medical environment, others in an office or even in retail. Some people like working artistically (such as a hairdresser or illustrator) while others prefer mental tasks (such as data manipulation or working with figures).

Pulled together, this information can provide a list of careers that capitalize on these strengths so that you now have a range of career options that would work for you. Not everyone is offered this advice at school and therefore if you suspect you are not in the right job or career, even if there is a charge for this service, it is worth considering to ensure you have access to the best advice – after all, this is your life, and you want to be working to your strengths not pulling away from them.

THE BENEFITS OF HAVING A PLANNED CAREER

You are probably thinking: why all the planning? After all, you probably bought this book because you wanted to find ways of making your current job more satisfying and here we are going back to basics, and considering events that happened a long time ago. We can't change the past – or can we?

The benefits of having a planned career rather than a career that literally skitters all over the place are numerous. Career planning:

- ▶ gives a focus to work towards and also helps with decision-making at a later date
- ▶ increases your motivation – you now have a drive and purpose for any courses you may decide to attend

- ▶ allows you to see where you want to end up – you can visualize an ultimate goal
- ▶ enables you to receive feedback and refine your behaviour within the planning framework of your career.

It is never too late to start planning and we can start right now. Look at Activity 2 in Part four of this book. You will see that it asks you to list all the jobs you have undertaken over a period of time, and then to find the threads of commonality that run through all of them. Let's think about this for a minute. I hinted earlier in this chapter that maybe you can change the past. What I meant by this is that we can pull together jobs that are seemingly unconnected and make them appear to form part of a career path. For example, perhaps years ago you worked on a market stall and then you went into a customer telephone call centre. At first these seem unconnected but in this example the career path is in communicating or interacting with the public. Were you good at it? Did you enjoy it? If so, then perhaps this could be part of your career path that should underpin any future decisions. Let's look at another example. Perhaps you had worked in a pub, later on at a betting shop and then at a bank. There are three strands here that immediately show themselves:

- ▶ Communicating with the public
- ▶ Working with figures
- ▶ Customer care.

Another point to mention is that the commonality may not be in the job role but in the industry. For example, you can hold many completely different jobs in local government and still consider your career path as being in the public sector.

When you start to think in this way, you will see that there is a clear path that you can find through even the most disparate CV. You literally might even have had a career path all the time, without knowing it!

The immediate benefit of this activity is that it forms a 'bigger picture' of your career path and therefore when you next meet someone and they ask you what you do for a living, you can reply, 'I have always worked with children' – or whatever your path may be. It also makes it much easier should you apply for a future job. When the interviewer asks you, 'Why don't you start by talking me through your career to date' you can begin by saying, 'Although my previous jobs may appear to be different they do in fact follow a career path of working closely with the public [or whatever].' This creates the illusion of planning when perhaps there had been none, and shows the interviewer that you have thought about the key aspects of your work, and how they flow into the job you are now seeking.

CV IN THE DRAWER OR A WORKING DOCUMENT?

This leads us to consider your Curriculum Vitae (CV). A CV is a document that charts your qualifications, skills and experience, and is often requested when an employer wants to assess your working history. Also, many professions now require a record of continuous professional development (CPD) to be maintained so that you can demonstrate how up to date you are in your profession. Elements of your CPD can also feature in your CV. With computers now the norm for most people, there really is no excuse not to be up to date and have the relevant documents to hand. However, be honest, is your CV a working document that you review regularly and have at your fingertips just in case an interesting opportunity arises, or is it languishing in a drawer, dusty and out of date? Imagine if someone walked up to you now with the opportunity of a lifetime – but only if you can give them your up-to-date CV right now. How would you fare? Would you be in a strong position to impress, or be found hiding in the corner, cursing at another wasted opportunity that only other people seem to get?

How you keep your CV is a good indication of how you view your future. The example of an opportunity depending on an up-to-date CV is not as farfetched as you might imagine. Maintaining a current CV in a professional format is not only important in case of an opportunity but it also helps you feel prepared and ready. You will feel more confident simply for having it there, in the wings, waiting. If you are unsure about how to create a CV, use Activity 24 in Part four of this book to help you.

Who stole my mojo?

If you are starting to get the impression that moulding your career involves activities and thought, then you are right. Unfortunately, often at the very time we need our mojo to keep us going it appears to have been stolen. We feel flat, low in spirits and worthless. We may even go on a journey of self-loathing, telling ourselves, 'Well, I can't be much good to have found myself in this position.' **If this is you, stop that right now!** Thinking like this helps no one and you will be working to confirm your worse fears.

The truth is that thinking negatively depletes energy and spirit. It is widely acknowledged that, 'as you think, so you will be'. The person who sits in the cage, convinced there is no way out, never questioning how they got in there in the first place, will become a victim of their situation.

It is true that to get you to where you want to be will take effort and energy. In other words you will only get out what you put in, and therefore if you truly want to learn how to carve out a career path that will be both satisfying and move in the direction you want to move in, then you will need to invest energy (e), effort (e) and time (t).

$$e + e + t = a \text{ (action)}$$

ENERGY

Nothing in the world moves without energy. Energy is found even in rock deposits, and it is fundamental to the laws of nature. You too run on energy. However, sometimes we feel more energetic and fired up than at other times. Harnessing our personal energy and using it for best effect is a skill that many could learn, but for now we want to maintain or even increase our motivational energy to enable us to plan our next move.

Setbacks reduce our energy. If you are feeling low in energy after being told that your job is being considered for redundancy, that is totally understandable, but you must not let the energy remain low for too long. You will need it to work on a future plan for yourself.

Extra energy can be found in a number of ways, and because we are all very different people, some of these ways will appeal to certain people more than others. You can garner energy in a number of ways including:

▶ Exercise – For some people, exercise is a great energy enhancer. If this is you, then you need to start a new regime or adjust the one you currently have to include more energy-inducing activities. Before you think this is just about hitting the gym, a good way to start is to just think about taking in some extra air by going for a long walk. Increasing your exercise in this way need not cost a fortune and of course it also has other benefits, such as toning your whole body. You will also feel more in touch with your environment than when you are a driver or passenger.

▶ Food intake – When you think about the foods you eat do you consciously think about the energy-giving properties of different foods? Fast foods are called that for one reason – they are fast. They are prepared quickly, cooked quickly and designed to be eaten in the minimum space or time or even on the go. They do not pretend to have great nutritional value or feed the body in the way that a carefully prepared meal might do, mainly because they are not supposed to replace regular eating. They are quick and easy for the occasional times when you need them – but they are not supposed to form a regular menu. Food is the fuel of the body. Good quality input will look after your inner engine and enable you to function far more effectively. Start gently by going back to basics and increasing the amount of fruit and vegetables you eat. They tone the body from the inside by keeping the whole gastric cycle working, and will provide you with valuable vitamins and anti-oxidants, to protect you from illness. When you begin to feel the benefits of this subtle change in diet, start looking at all other aspects of what you eat and when you eat. We can easily fall into lazy eating habits that sap our energy and ruin our self-esteem.

▶ Energy drinks – These are great for giving you a quick pick-up if you need to do something fast (such as run a marathon or write a report) but not really suitable for long-term use as the body gets used to the ingredients and then more is needed to create the same effect. Also the increased energy is not sustained for long, and the 'high' produced can become a 'low' later on. Instead, think in terms of more natural energy drinks such as making your own berry or banana smoothies. They may take a little more effort but not only will they give you natural energy but they will also stave off any hunger pangs, and keep you satisfied for longer.

▶ Vitamins, minerals and supplements – You can buy a whole range of vitamins and supplements from health food stores and chemists, but if you are eating thoughtfully you should not need many of these to supplement your diet. However, for the times when we are working flat out and eating on the go, or just need that extra bit of energy, there are many supplement compounds on the market. These offer you a carefully controlled combination of vitamins and minerals to target specific symptoms. They may be worth considering if you are in a pressured situation, but you should not rely on them for long-term use.

▶ Social energy – This comes from, for example, doing a hobby you like or meeting with friends. Have you ever felt tired after work but somehow you find the energy to go to your evening class or club and you miraculously come alive? You will find that when you are undertaking an activity you enjoy you will have a surge of energy. You will never feel more energetic sitting on the sofa watching TV – energy begets energy (which is why exercise works). The key here is to find a social activity that you enjoy, whether that is salsa dancing or stamp collecting, and then mix with like-minded people. Even without the activity, people give off energy too. Therefore, if you are not into hobbies but just like conversation, find yourself some enthusiastic friends to energize you.

▶ Colours and environment – Colour therapy has been shown to affect our moods and restore energy. Blue is known to be relaxing, yellow induces happiness, green is thought a good colour for learning, and red can cause excitement! If you exist in a beige colour scheme, try to bring some colour into your life. You may not be allowed to paint the walls at work but you can choose your colour scheme at home, introduce colourful flowers on your desk, or brighten the clothes you wear socially.

▶ Environmental factors – Our environment can also increase or reduce energy. Some people are energized by beautiful countryside, others by the sea. You may not be able to live or work in your favoured environment but you can have pictures with you to draw your energy from. Next time you are feeling tired in a room, rather than blame your situation look around you and see what you can deduce from the environment. Perhaps your environment is part of the problem – and there may be something you can do about that!

EFFORT

This really is very simple. The laws of physics state that if you put effort into something, you will get something out. (I think my forebears would have phrased it as, 'You don't get 'owt for nowt' – but the sentiment is the same.) This does not mean clearing the decks for some supreme venture, but it does mean undertaking some of the activities featured in Part four of this book. Investing some quality thought in where you are going and some soul searching in making sure you are heading in the right direction for you.

Careers very rarely fall in people's laps, and your chosen career may mean that you need to undertake additional qualifications, move to a different area or move into a new business altogether – all things that require effort on your part. Are you prepared for this? Do you have the energy in place to help you with the effort of changing your focus? When it comes to your career, your considerations may need to be quite egocentric (that is, concerned with you and no one else). To undertake the effort required you need to ask yourself: How much do I really want this? And also: Who can help and support me with this? (See Activities 12 and 14 in Part four of this book for help with an action plan and motivation).

TIME

The amount of time it can take to get on the right track for your career will vary. If you are looking at a promotion within your current business, you may have to take on additional responsibilities, and prove yourself over a period of time. That could be six months or a few years. However, if you are considering changing your career completely, then you might need to consider new qualifications or an apprenticeship which could take years to achieve. Both of these examples require focused activities that take time, and therefore you need to become highly time-conscious and time-efficient. How have you been spending your time so far? Could that time be used more efficiently? Depending on the amount of time you need to free up to achieve these, try the following:

▶ Keep a time log – See Activity 3 in Part four of this book. Until you are aware of where you are spending your time, you cannot know how and what to change.

▶ Doubling up – Try to identify times in the day where you could perhaps double up some activities. For example, if you needed to find a way to study for a particular qualification you could listen to learning course materials while you are travelling to work or jogging in the park instead of your usual music. Or you could read some learning materials/books while you are engaged in 'dead-time' situations such as when sitting in a waiting room while your child has their ballet or piano lesson.

▶ Rota time – We all love to be needed but you may be wasting time if you always appear available at every minute of the day. Carve out some time away from the family – it might only be one hour a week, but think what you could achieve in that time. Be fair and create a rota whereby everyone has their evening or portion of time when they do their own thing. You might find it becomes a pleasant habit.

▶ Ask for additional time – If you are in an industry that is downsizing, you may be able to ask your manager for some time out to undertake a career change. When redundancies are threatening, some organizations will allow staff to go on courses, work with a job coach and take additional time to study in the hope that they will be able to find another job quickly, but this is not a given for every organization so be aware that your request may not be granted.

When leaving is not an option

The career market is like any other, full of ups and downs. There are times when jobs are easier to come by and conversely times when it is difficult to find the type of job you want. Some organizations only recruit once a year and if you are waiting for a specific job to come up you might be waiting for some time. This can be compounded by the fact that when times are tough, and consumer confidence is lacking, many people seem to lay low in the job they are in. In other words, people feel less sure of trying out new ventures. They stay put and this results in less movement in the market. In addition the economic climate fluctuates and can have a dramatic effect on certain industries.

This can be very frustrating for you, the keen worker, who wants to prove their ability in a new career or feels ready for promotion. You want to scale the heights, but someone has taken the ladder away and blocked the lift!

I could sympathize with your situation over a cup of coffee but that is not really going to help, is it? You want action and you want it now. Well, action might just be closer than you think.

The important point here is to consider what you can change and what is out of your control. Complete Activity 4 (in Part four of this book) and this will inform you of the factors that are within your control and those that are not. When factors are within our control we can actively move them forward; however, when they appear not to be within our control we have to firstly break them down (as there may be certain elements that actually are within our control, and that we can do something about) and then find a way of accepting and coping with those elements that remain. For example, you may covet a certain role in the company but there is someone in that role and they do not appear to be moving anywhere. You may not be able to push them out of the job but you can make sure that you have all the skills in readiness for the job when (and if) it does come up. That might leave you thinking, 'But I still can't make them leave. I still can't control that element.' No, but you can look at similar jobs within your company, or ones that share a similar discipline. Some jobs share basic background skills that you can attain and then you can move sideways when the opportunity arises. Also, the person within the original job may need an assistant. This would be a good career move for you, even if it is not exactly what you want. You can learn 'on the job', and many assistants are promoted into their manager's job when the opportunity arises.

SKILLING AND RE-SKILLING

One thing is clear from this example: staying still and wishing from a distance, without any action, is unlikely to impress at the recruitment stage. Saying 'I have been waiting for this job opportunity for the past three years' and then clearly showing that you have done nothing towards ensuring you are fully skilled and ready to walk into the opportunity will slide you down the scale of applicants rather than move you upwards.

When you gain new skills you are not just doing this for employment – you are investing in yourself, and that brings with it a certain pride and satisfaction. From this point of view you may indeed decide to pay for some learning, given that you will always have the evidence on your CV and that the certificate will be in your toolbox and at your disposal for the rest of your life.

In some instances organizations may offer staff a number of training programmes to attend, or are willing to help staff seek training outside of work. If they are helping you to find programmes that do not link to your work, be prepared that this may not be paid for by your organization, and therefore you will need to think through how you will fund this – but do be open to any help available, even if it is time off to attend. If the organization you work for has a training function they can help you with locating the right courses for you. The important thing is not to focus on gaining qualifications (unless you need them for a professional job) but on skills.

VOLUNTEERING

When the wait seems interminable you will need a focus that takes you away from the workplace and into a position that can make you smile. Many organizations now support volunteering as a positive way of helping you gain skills that help the community. (If your boss needs persuading, it is also great advertising for the company.) Find out about the volunteering opportunities in your area. They can be a great way of lifting your frustrations while also helping you gain skills. Many employers are very keen on employing staff who have undertaken the Duke of Edinburgh scheme – not because of the badge but because of the skills that the programme propagates such as team leadership, organization, time management and self-motivation. You may be too old to undertake an award scheme like this but you can equally gain these skills through contributing to volunteering projects. Do some fast research and you may find that your organization already supports a school or local group that you can work with. This will raise the profile of your organization as well as increasing your skills.

Recapturing your original motivation

In the previous section we discussed when leaving is not always possible and explored some practical measures you can take so that you move forwards while essentially standing still in the same job. However, while you are in this position you still need to maintain your motivation (and/or passion). Therefore this needs some consideration.

Motivate: to act in a particular way, stimulate interest

(taken from *The Concise Oxford Dictionary*)

All managers and organizations work together to provide some level of motivation for their staff. This could be in the form of a pay scheme, free drinks, days off, flexible working hours and/or bonus schemes. However, motivation is not 100% up to your employer; every employee also has a duty to motivate themselves.

Firstly, let's think about why you took this job in the first place. Perhaps you felt that it was the first foothold on the rung of a particular industry, perhaps your friend works there, or maybe you just saw it offered and thought it was interesting, or local. Whatever your reason, that formed your first motivation and became the impetus for applying for that role.

Fast-forward to the present day and now that you want to make a move into another role you feel that your job no longer motivates you and that the real motivation lies with the next move. Great – except, what if there is no next move? At this stage you can start to feel very demotivated if you're not careful. You start to feel like you are treading water. You are still working to increase your skills base and you are still focused on where you want to be – but something is lacking emotionally. Basically you need to fall in love with your job again. Remember the excitement you felt when you were initially offered your job? Where has that gone, and who (or what) is responsible for it disappearing?

Remotivating yourself takes some dedication as it is always far easier to find the faults in anything than finding the good points. So many jobs seem exciting until you work within the industry. (It is a bit like finding out how a magic trick is done – it loses its ability to amaze when you are in on the act.) However, having that inside knowledge does not mean that the magic is lost forever; you just need a more current variation of the trick to be enchanted again. Remotivating yourself is about rediscovering that magic again in your job.

Insight

Close your eyes for a moment and re-experience your first feelings about getting your current job. Open your eyes and write three words that express that feeling.

Is that excitement still there? If so, has it become dormant (and how could you re-energize it)? If not, what new developments lie ahead that could excite you?

When you feel low in motivation your confidence also takes a knock back. It is not uncommon to question whether it is you that is not able to deal with the lack of opportunity or is failing in some way – even though the economic or market situation is the real reason. A crisis in confidence can certainly block your ability to remotivate. To help you, work through Activity 5 – 'Affirmation and confirmation' (in Part four of this book) – and start practising immediately.

What does your CV say about you?

Remember we discussed your CV earlier? Well, now is the time to really look at how you are selling yourself!

Think about this for a moment: What does the current state of your CV say about you? If you don't have your CV up to date and to hand, are you really serious about moving jobs? There is a saying that, 'opportunity opens the door to those who go knocking', but if you are not ready to 'go knocking' because you don't have a 'killer' CV then you might just be fooling yourself. If you are unsure about how to create a CV, go to Activity 24 – 'Creating a killer CV' – in Part four of this book.

YOUR CV

Your CV is an organized, written presentation of what you offer – not simply an outline of your job description. Ultimately it is a sales brochure and you are the product. CVs are not only used when applying for a new job; they can also be used as 'introducers' at networking meetings or attached to project work or bidding paperwork.

When people ask to see your CV they want to see a life story in brief. They also expect to see some form of progression or continuity – a thread running through the document (see Activity 2 – 'Through the time tunnel'). If you don't have this then your CV could look a little chaotic and lacking focus.

Your CV should be:

▶ Easy to read – This does not mean over-simplistic language, but refrain from fancy fonts or confusing colour combinations. It should never be more than two pages long.

- ▶ Eye catching – Experiment with different quality papers and inks. You need your CV to appeal to all the senses.
- ▶ Well laid out – Incorporate plenty of white space around your words and view the whole document as if you were setting out a page in a magazine – does it look balanced?
- ▶ Original and interesting – You cannot put everything in a CV and therefore you need to be selective. You want to stimulate the reader's interest so that they want to meet you to find out more, rather than try to tell them everything in one document.
- ▶ Relevant – You may need to refocus your CV for every job you apply for. This does not mean bending the truth, it simply means promoting specific aspects of your experience that may be more relevant for each particular job.
- ▶ Strong – Your CV may be considered alongside other contenders. You need to stand out and therefore use positive, strong language.
- ▶ Factual and believable – *Never* lie on a CV, you will be found out. Ensure your dates are correct and that the information you give is believable. For example, if you undertook two jobs at the same time, make this clear, otherwise the reader will think you had your dates confused.
- ▶ Concise – Your CV should never be more than two pages. People just do not have time to read beyond this length.
- ▶ Selling your strengths and abilities – This is a selling document and so make sure you sell yourself to the reader. Also only include skills and abilities pertaining to the position you covet – no one is interested in your great knitting ability unless it is relevant to the job.
- ▶ Matching the current job market – If you are not sure what skills and abilities are required for the job then find out and make sure your CV matches.

There are two main formats for CVs:

- ▶ Reverse chronology – This is the most traditional form of CV. Basically, after your personal details, you are listing your previous jobs, starting with your most recent. (The reason for displaying your jobs in reverse order is that your most current job is the one in which you have most recent experience.) Reverse chronology is excellent for showing flow and how the skills from one position led onto another. However, it is not so good if you have had many jobs as the long list draws attention to this, and that may be off-putting to an employer.

▶ Functional – This is where you create your CV around the various functions of a job, giving examples from multiple employers in each section. CVs written in this way also do not always have dates. For example, you may have a heading 'Financial acumen' and under that cite three different employers where you proved your financial acumen ('While working for James and Partners I ... and while at Smith and Sons I ...'). This technique allows you to concentrate on the skills they need while providing evidence for each from several jobs. Another advantage of using functional headings is if your career is a little muddled and does not show a strong progression. These aspects become hidden in a functional format.

These are demonstrated in more detail in Activity 24.

PHOTO OR NO PHOTO?

Should you include a photo on your CV? This very much depends on how you intend using the CV. When sending it to another company this might be a good idea because they will be able to identify you easily when you come into the building. However, if you are handing around copies of your CV at a networking event, you risk the fact that it might appear slightly pretentious.

CREATING A PERSONAL PROFILE

Personal profiles are a great way to build on your CV. If you have a great deal of experience that may not come through in your CV, and remember the golden rule of no more than two pages – well, sometimes that is just not enough. Attach a personal profile and it is another document, so you can say more without adding more pages to your CV.

What does a personal profile look like? Well, here it is perfectly acceptable to add a photo to accompany the text. As for what to write, imagine you are either sending a press release about yourself to a newspaper or that someone is interviewing you. Write in the third person, for example, 'Sylvia has worked in the care industry for ten years', and provide any information that does not sit well in a CV. It can be personal, 'Trevor has two cats and lives in Upminster', or passionate, 'Alison has always enjoyed working with people, and this has been the basis of her previous employment.'

If you are at all concerned with including a personal profile with your CV, especially as it was not requested, use a light touch and tell the recipient (in person or by letter), 'I hope you don't mind but I have also enclosed a personal profile that I wrote for another client. I have included it for your interest.' For more details about creating a personal profile see Activity 25 in Part four of this book.

What do you say about you?

We are all walking, talking adverts for ourselves and rightly or wrongly people make assumptions regarding our potential and decisions about whether we are suitable for a certain position or not based on how we look and conduct ourselves.

Take a good, long look in the mirror. Have you been guilty of letting this part of your image down? Do you find that you are dressing for comfort rather than impact? Comfort is fine if you are happy to stay in your current role, but if that were the case I would guess that you would not be reading this book.

Your image and style will be discussed in Part two of this book, but for now I want you to think about the overall message your image is promoting. Some key questions to ask yourself are:

▶ How smartly do I dress?
▶ Do I know for certain that the colours I wear really suit me?
▶ Have I become used to wearing one or two items constantly, just because they are 'easy'?
▶ Am I blending into the background?

Now consider what your answers say about you. Quite often we settle into wearing a uniform of our own making without realizing that to everyone else this screams a lack of interest in ourselves, our job or a lack of self-esteem – none of which is good. You may be communicating that you feel your life is in a rut without ever opening your mouth, just through your body language and clothes.

I SAY!

What do you actually say about yourself? We will discuss conduct in a minute but when a colleague (or a potential employer) asks you about yourself what do you say? Do you put yourself down, 'I am only the typist', or do you give yourself more worth by describing yourself as, 'a key member of the customer relations team'? We also need to think about whether we use repetitive phrases and annoying speech inflections (discussed in more detail in the following section). Would you really like to get stuck in a lift with yourself?

How we talk about ourselves matters. It gives off volumes of information to the other person not only in the words we use but also *how* we say things. It can be difficult to spot this in ourselves, so ask others for feedback on this aspect of your presentation. Voice coaches can help you work to create a more authoritative or assertive tone if needed.

BODY TALK

Let's turn our attention to body talk, and I don't mean just walking around.

▶ Pay some attention to how you sit if you sit at a computer or desk – Poor sitting technique can result in sore and tired shoulders, which in turn create bad posture.
▶ Check out your chair – You should be sitting in a chair that can be adjusted to your height and weight.
▶ Look at your desk – A desk is for working on, not storing papers, so make sure you have a clear area to work on. Your desk may also be adjustable, and if it is then check out the settings.
▶ Adjust your workstation – If you have a computer on your desk, make sure that the screen is of the right height and tilt for you to work comfortably. Where is your keyboard situated? Do you need a wrist support?

Ensuring your basic position is supported will enable you to maintain a good posture that you will then take with you when you move around the workplace.

Now let's consider how you move around. From time to time it is good to move from any static position, otherwise you are in danger of developing poor postural habits. Start to consider:

► how you move from a seated position to a standing one
► whether you move with a heavy tread or a light one
► how you reach out and grab items (such as the telephone)
► the extent to which you knock into things
► the way in which you walk from one side of the workplace to the other.

Moving with style and grace is not necessarily a natural gift. Everyone can train themselves to move with more consideration for their body. Were you to take up dancing, then you would need to consider not only every aspect of how your body moves but also how that movement is perceived by others. In other words what messages that movement sends to others.

When people watch you move around, they will make assumptions about you, your level in the organization and how efficient and effective you are. It may seem unfair but it is true and you need to consider carefully how you appear to others if you are to design yourself a new, more confident image.

Insight

Imagine you are in a movie of your life. What conclusions would the viewer make about the way you move and sit at work? Who would you ask to play you in this movie and why? Imagine that the character in the movie suddenly becomes successful – how would you ask the actor playing you to depict you now?

CARRYING EXTRA PAPERS OR EQUIPMENT

From time to time you will need to carry paperwork or equipment around. Again, how do you do this? Are you someone battling with mountains of paper that looks as if it is about to fall out of your arms, or do you have a way of organizing work in folders so that you look positively in control? Does your handbag or briefcase bulge at the seams or do they close easily, giving the appearance of being smart and professional? Think about the image you portray – would you be happy to leave a project with someone who does not seem to be able to organize their own briefcase or bag? I rest my case. Get out your bag (or look at your desk) and sort it out now.

MEETING AND GREETING

The first time we meet anyone in any situation, we automatically create assumptions about them – it is an annoying but natural phenomenon that happens nearly every time. Therefore the way that we meet and greet work colleagues can be hugely influential in our future quest. Start practising now by looking up Activity 7 in Part four of this book and design an introduction that excites and interests the other party – and start using it, straight away. It is never too soon to create the right impression.

Would you really like to be stuck in a lift with yourself?

We all collect habits as we go through our work life, and I am sure you can think of several colleagues who irritate and annoy you for any number of reasons – but what if we are that person to someone else? How do we know that we are not as annoying to others?

MIRROR, MIRROR ON THE WALL

It is time to take a good, long, hard look at ourselves in the mirror and see ourselves for who and what we are. In the previous section we looked at how you have been presenting yourself to others in terms of your visual impact and your introduction. However, it did not address the subject of mannerisms and behaviour.

First of all, let's look at repetitive words and phrases. Using one word or phrase repeatedly can be very annoying. Become very aware of words that are fine on their own, such as 'OK', but become very annoying when they litter every sentence. Check your language for modern slang such as 'innit', and phrases that become 'habitual confetti' scattered regularly throughout your speech (for example, 'you know what I mean?'). These phrases are usually easy to identify because they add nothing to the meaning of the sentence but speak volumes about your lack of clear communication. They often appear when the speaker is nervous and are used as a verbal 'comfort blanket' to soothe the speaker, but unfortunately, rather than disguise nerves, they emphasize them. The constant repetition then becomes an irritant to the listener and that prevents good communication.

Other common speech problems include mumbling, snorting at the end of a sentence, inappropriate laughing and reverting to child-like behaviour and speech. These behaviours are particularly prevalent when someone is speaking to a person in authority, or in a stressful situation (such as during a presentation). You are not at school now but it is surprising how many people do this because it is learned behaviour from childhood.

Mannerisms can also become very annoying and/or inappropriate. These often become magnified when you are put in a stressful situation, such as having to present to a customer or a large number of people. Whirling hand gestures and the pulling of strange faces may go down well when you are telling a story in the pub, but become highly inappropriate in business. In the same way as we need feedback on other aspects of our work, try to gain some feedback as to how you have been presenting yourself. The good news is that most mannerisms are habitual and can easily be unlearned so if something is revealed, don't worry about it – learn to change it.

UNLEARNING AN ANNOYING HABIT

Habits are a form of learned behaviour, and therefore it is quite easy to minimize or remove them completely by undertaking four easy stages.

The first stage of changing this behaviour is to face up to the fact that we do it. We need to acknowledge we have this habit and recognize how annoying it can be to others. From the point of acknowledging it, the behaviour has moved from our unconscious and into our conscious, in other words we are aware every time we do it. Fantastic – now we are aware of our behaviour, we can do something about it.

The second stage of changing a habit is to recognize that the habit has come from some form of anxiety. For example, if the habit is that you find it difficult to look your manager in the eye when you talk to them, this behaviour has come from your anxiety at what your manager might say or do. This could have emerged from something your manager once said or it could even be from some childhood memory linked to a senior figure in your life. Anxiety is a form of protection and therefore it is a natural defence but if it is getting in the way of other things you want to achieve then it needs addressing. Look at Activity 8 in Part four of this book for ways to reduce anxiety in general.

The third stage of changing a habit is to replace the unwanted behaviour with a more helpful one. Going back to our example, if you are having trouble making eye contact with your manager, look slightly above their eyes, so that you are looking at their eyebrows. You will still give the impression of looking at them but you have just made the action a lot easier for yourself.

The final stage is to practise so that you become more comfortable with the new body language while also developing and working with your skills so that you start to receive good feedback on your manner.

THE ART OF BEING INTERESTING

People like to converse with people who are interesting and have something to say. This does not mean that you have to jabber on to everyone who crosses your path, but is it important to have a conversation-starter hidden in your toolbox. Imagine you really were stuck in that lift – would you want to stand there silently or would someone with a good conversing style help the time to go by?

Consider for a moment:

- ▶ who you talk to
- ▶ what you talk about
- ▶ whether it is light banter or interesting topics
- ▶ whether you speak positively or run life, the company and the world, down?

All of these factors affect the image you present and how seriously you are taken at work.

A tip – If you are stuck at this point and are thinking, 'How can I make my conversation more interesting?' always remember that people (generally) love to talk about themselves. As soon as you feel stuck, push the conversation over to the other person, for example:

Colleague: Did you have a good weekend?

You: Yes, good thanks, but tell me about yours. Did you manage to get out with the family? I want to hear all about it!

Or

Colleague: What is it really like working in Fosters?

You: It's fun, but tell me about what your company is doing this Christmas … are you still having the traditional party?

The trick is that you appear to be a great conversationalist and very interesting to talk to, even though they have done most of the talking!

2

Starting to plan for the future

In this chapter you will learn:
- *how to begin to prepare mentally*
- *how to assess your skills*
- *how to create an action plan*

Our minds can be so powerful and we can harness that power to great effect, as we will see later on. However, mind power can also work against us and we can suddenly find it sneaking in and limiting our options. Try to be ever aware of the need to defeat the monster mindset.

Battling the monster mindset

When you start to think in terms of moving your job, there is a danger that suddenly you think of your current job as being negative. This can then be reflected in your speech and you find yourself saying, 'If only they did this here', or 'I'm never included in ...' The danger of this route is that:

▶ It is often untrue – We have already said how much easier it is to be negative than positive, and because things are not happening the way you want, is it always the organization's fault? Could you have instigated the thing that is missing, or could you ask to be included in future activities?

▶ It becomes a negative, downward spiral of despair – What if the country (or your industry) is caught in a downturn and there are no jobs in your industry 'out there'? You will have to remain in your current job for the time being but you will feel dissatisfied. Dissatisfaction is the curse of development because it threatens to suck you into a mire of negativity, where the only victim is you.

I am sure you have heard the saying 'the grass is always greener on the other side'? Well, it isn't! You may indeed go looking at other fields later on but you need to make peace with the field you are in before you leave. Over the years I have met so many people who have told me that life would be so much better if they could just get over this problem or over that situation – but guess what? They achieve their goal and then meet yet another situation or problem. This does not mean that anyone should stay put and not strike out, but when you move on how much more healthy is it to move on with an honest heart rather than feeling you are sneaking away?

We think pink when we think back to previous jobs we have had. I am sure some of you will don those rose-tinted spectacles and decide that it was not so bad there after all – in fact, come to think of it, you don't know why you left. Humans have an annoying habit of doing this. We forget the pain of the situation at the time and remember only the good bits. It is another defence mechanism and similarly we expect those problems not to be in the next job. The truth is that all jobs have good and bad aspects – what's important is whether you care to focus on them and give them your attention, or let them drift.

A negative mindset is a dangerously powerful spiral that can suck you down and incarcerate you in a world of gloom of your own making.

To experience the power of your mindset in action, try this experiment. Get up tomorrow morning and (whatever the weather or circumstance) tell yourself that today is a great day. Give yourself permission to feel really happy. Say 'hello' to everyone and be very upbeat. Whatever happens to you during the day look on the sunny side and make the day fun. At the end of the day write down a summary of your day and give it a rating out of ten.

The following day undertake the same exercise but tell yourself that today is a horrible day, you don't want to go to work because you hate your job, nobody likes you and you are not appreciated. At the end of the day write down the summary of your day again and give it a rating out of ten.

Now compare the two summaries. It is likely that in the first you used positive language and saw the good aspects of the day (you might even have written that you were happy that you actually had a job to go to). In the second it is likely that you used very negative language and even minor things irritated you. You may even have written, 'I don't like my job and want to move.'

What is remarkable is that the two days were probably little different – it was your attitude on each day that changed. Your car failing to start might spell disaster on the negative day but be seen as a way of having another coffee and spending less time in the office on the more positive day.

For more on how to break through a static mindset see Activities 9 and 10 in Part four of this book.

Now, apply this thinking to your current job. Is it really that bad? Spend a week being positive about your employer and then decide whether moving positions is the best idea for you. It is possible to fall back in love with the job you already have, and in an economic downturn or when you are constrained by other factors, it can put your career back on track.

Assessing your skills

We are now approaching the end of Part one, and hopefully you will be more aware of yourself and the psychological drivers making you want to move your career forward or even in a totally different direction. However large a role positive thinking takes in creating the 'can do' attitude that will take you forward, you will also need solid skills. Think of your skills as being the underpinning foundation of your work. Someone recruiting for a job will want to know that you come with a certain amount of knowledge and ability, and that is where your proven skills come in. List your skills under three headings as shown in Activity 11 in Part four of this book:

▶ Qualifications – These are the skills for which you have been assessed and given an award. Many qualifications (although not all) are knowledge based. This means that the certificate may only prove that you understand the background to certain concepts. For example, if you undertook a management qualification in college the qualification may show that you *know* how to deal with a difficult member of the team, but it does not prove that you can actually *do* this in practice. For this reason, qualifications are only part of the picture.

▶ Vocational skills and qualifications – These are awards that are given for demonstrating that you have actually undertaken various situations. They are often in a portfolio of narrative and confirmed by a manager who provides the credibility. Continuing the example mentioned under 'Qualifications', you would need to show by writing a narrative that you have actually dealt effectively with a difficult member of staff, including the method you used, the outcome and any learning points. It shows any future employer that you have actually done this, but of course if you do not have someone difficult to deal with then achieving every aspect of these awards can be a little more difficult.

▶ Life skills – Our learning does not begin and end in the workplace. There are numerous opportunities outside of work to acquire skills that are valuable and can be extended into work. Perhaps you have done some voluntary work, or maybe you are involved in local politics, sit on a committee or have a small part-time job. Have you ever been a governor for a school or undertaken some adult education programmes? These are all skills you can bring to the table, build on in future and make you the person you are. Think laterally: if you have ever brought up children, then you surely have negotiating skills. These are transferable skills. At this stage write everything down as you think of it. It can always be refined at a later point when you are in a position to put your skills forward on a CV or application form.

TRANSFERABLE SKILLS

As mentioned in the previous section, transferable skills are skills that can be transferred from one activity in order to demonstrate another activity. In the example we said that if a job required negotiation skills then the ability to deal with a large family of individuals could demonstrate that ability. Similarly, if the job required you to be able to manage a team but you had not done that in your previous job, then you might be able to put forward another example such as running a scout group or club. Transferable skills are very real and are taken seriously by recruiters but should only be used when a more accurate match is not available.

Creating an action plan

Let's reflect on what we have covered so far. The focus of this part of the book is to help you think about how you came to be in your current situation and ascertain whether there may be possibilities for growing within that role, or whether you wish to move on. We did this by considering:

► what a career is and how it actually defines us
► the energy you need to even consider making a change
► how to feel fulfilled even if moving is not an option
► how to be self-motivated
► what your CV says about you
► how to recognize your behaviours
► how to create the right mindset for change
► taking a skills assessment.

All of these topics were accompanied by activities laid out in Part four of this book. The activities are there to enable you to gain a greater understanding of yourself through each topic, and to apply the thinking to your own individual circumstance. Our individuality guarantees that each of us will gain different outcomes from these activities, and some of the outcomes may be enlightening, so please take the time to do these if you are able. If you feel the urge to hop over them, resist it if you can because the thought processes that they excite will enable you to consider the reality of your career and its future prospects in depth.

However, reflecting is only one aspect of considering your career. To make things happen you need *action* and to make sure you stay focused along the way you need an *action plan*.

YOUR ACTION PLAN

First, let's do the sum:

ideas + action = change

If we need to make changes in our career world we need to have not just the ideas (or thought processes) but also the action of doing something with them. In other words, ideas are great but they stay as just ideas without the action of implementing them. This may seem simple but that final 'call to action' is one of the most difficult aspects of this process. For example, consider the process of writing a book. Many people feel that they can do this: they mentally plot a great storyline, or think their way through the topic, but do they ever get started – sadly, on many occasions, the answer is no. Quite often fear is the main protagonist that stops you doing what you want to do in life, and you may not even be aware of it. It is usually:

▶ Fear of the unknown – What if I give all this up for a new career that I don't really know anything about? My job might be boring but it is comfortable and safe.
▶ Fear of failure – What if I try but fail in my new career? Will people laugh at me? Will I look foolish for trying?
▶ Fear of taking on too much – What if it all becomes too much for me? What will happen if I cannot undertake all that travelling (or studying)?

My answer to all of these fears is that you need to think of your career as less of a destination that is set and more like a fluid river that might ebb and flow, and mould to the rules of nature. This way you should never feel bad about changing course again and again in your quest to find the right career or job for you. Each twist and turn provides experience and learning what we do not like takes us one step nearer to knowing what we want. As long as you learn along the way so that you can take those skills with you, you will find that those who have a lot of experience have a lot more to offer a future employer. However, if your fear paralyses you into inaction, you will only feel frustrated and annoyed with yourself, which can result in feeling stifled and negative.

One of the main problems with fear is that it escalates in no time from a trickle into a raging torrent that then becomes both suffocating and debilitating.

This is where a well-structured action plan can help, and the beauty of this technique is that you can set the progress at a pace that you feel comfortable with. Even baby steps will take you forward if you have planned the direction carefully. Look at Activity 12 in Part four of this book. It will show you how to draft out an action plan – don't forget to enter the other activities from this book into your plan so that you allow time for them too.

KEEPING YOUR ACTION PLAN

Make a diary date with yourself to check your action plan regularly. Make life easy for yourself by reviewing your action plan at the same time each week or each month. This will provide you with a trigger so that you do not forget. For example, you could choose:

► the first day of every month
► every Monday morning
► the 10th of every month.

Or you could choose to align it to another activity:

► every pay day
► every time you check your weight
► every morning while you wait for the train to arrive.

Regular checking will ensure you are constantly 'on the case' and have your future completely in focus at all times. This will become the template by which you make your decisions or apportion your time, and as such will help you with your time management. You will not want to waste time on other activities that do not take you further forwards, towards your goals – and each time you are able to achieve an activity, tick it off and reassess where you are on your journey and the next steps towards getting there.

For this reason, your action plan should be a living document that moves and changes to suit your timeframe and your life. You can change your action plan if you change your career aspirations – nothing is written in tablets of stone. This makes your plan flexible and easily adapted to whatever life throws at you.

Every time you look at your action plan you will be thinking, 'Is this what I want? Are my goals the same?' and therefore you will be reflecting on your decisions and realigning them at every juncture.

Insight

Reduce your action plan to bulleted points and write them on a card that you can carry around with you (as in Activity 5). You are more likely to read them (and therefore reflect and act on them) at regular intervals.

If you are more creative and visual and find linear lists do not suit your mode of thinking, try creating a 'Wish Life' collage. To do this, collect images and cut outs that represent where you want to be in your life and paste them onto a board. Place the board by your desk or in an area you visit regularly. It serves the same purpose as the memory cards in that it will enable you to keep your desired destination in focus at all times.

Just as in the action plan, don't be afraid to change its contents and images as you move forwards.

Case studies

CAROL

As Carol completes the first part of this book, she has learned a lot about herself and recognized how much she has put her family first. Now the family are grown, Carol recognizes that she is finally thinking of herself.

Carol wanted to think through why she has suddenly started to feel unsettled; after all, Morgan Pilchard has been very good to her and provided her with basic training, but she is starting to realize that perhaps she has conquered her job and needs to be stretched a little more.

Carol has made the decision that she will not leave Morgan Pilchard until she has worked her way through the book and decided on a clear route to follow. Although she feels quite confident in her work she does not feel very self-confident and therefore she also tries the 'Affirmation and confirmation' activity and finds it helpful. She also has to be honest in that she does not have a CV, and so sets about trying to write one.

SAMIA

Through undertaking the 'Through the time tunnel' activity, Samia sees that she was talked into joining the apprentice scheme offered by the factory with little thought. She also notices that there was another significant event at the same time: her grandmother died. Samia thinks that her deciding to take on the apprenticeship at that time was a reaction to the situation at home; she did not want to create any more problems and so took an action that seemed to please everyone. She now thinks that this may have been a mistake, but at least she can see that the job has given her a lot of experience.

The biggest decision Samia has made as a result of working through Part one is to take responsibility for her career. She must not wait for the decision of the organization, and there are certainly some aspects of the reorganization that she can control. This sudden realization has given her more energy and she is now looking around the organization to see what she can do, and create an action plan. Regarding her wedding she has set a date in her diary one month from now to review the whole situation. She has decided not to make any big decisions until then. Feeling organized has helped her to get on with her work as now she is organized and more in control of her situation than she was before.

JASON

Jason is already doing some soul searching. He has been thinking about his behaviour at school and how he probably was part of the problem. He also starts to realize that the only person who got him into this situation is himself, and only he can get himself out of it. In a way he is becoming more mature and realizes the implications of his actions. He realizes, when he reads further, that his behaviour probably leaves a lot to be desired and he admits that actually he would hate to be stuck in a lift with himself.

When Jason does the 'What your career says about you' activity he realizes that he does not want to be in that job in the future, but he is still unsure of what to do. He cannot afford to leave and go to college as he has taken out a loan to buy a car and needs his salary to make the monthly repayments. He is still feeling stuck but in his action plan he decides to think more about his behaviour and some ways in which he might personally change.

HENRI

Henri has been reflecting on his career when undertaking the 'Through the time tunnel' activity and has decided that, although there were many good times at the council, he must put this behind him now if he is going to move on. However, he also reflected on how and why he joined the council in the first place and realizes that it was an opening at a time when he needed a steady income. He starts to think that the job never really reflected his personality and was simply an office job. The more he thinks about this he feels that, although he needs another job to help pay university fees and to supplement Sarah's salary, with his redundancy pay he might not need to earn quite so much and possibly he should be looking in other directions. When you lose your job the temptation is to immediately try and find a similar job – but what if he went radical and did something completely different? The thought excites him and suddenly, rather than being morose, Henri is motivated to undertake further self-exploration. His mojo is back and suddenly the world seems to be his oyster.

CHRIS

Chris is having to accept that she did not leave her job, the job left her. There is little point in trying to find a position in another estate agency – she has tried and at the moment they are all in the same situation. Her confidence needs a boost and so she decides to undertake the 'Affirmation and confirmation' activity to make sure she does not lose belief in herself. She also decides to dust off a very old CV that still has her old address details on it! She starts to work on that as, after all, she will need it now that she is in the wider job market. She also practises the 'Meet and greet people with impact' activity because she now recognizes that new opportunities could be anywhere and she needs to be ready for them.

Chris is also realizing that at 35 she is still very young and she has plenty of time to think in terms of a totally new career. Suddenly she feels more in control again: she is more energized and enthusiastic, and is thinking less about scouring the paper for a job and more about what she actually wants to do. Retraining is something she had never thought of but suddenly it seems more interesting.

10 THINGS TO REMEMBER

1 Your career is in your hands. It is likely that you will work for a long time and so you must make the most of the time you have by deciding on a job or career that you find fulfilling.

2 You do not always need a new job to revitalize you – start by looking at what you already have.

3 You can fall 'in love' with a job again – it just takes a little romancing and remembering what you liked about the job in the first place.

4 You cannot be blamed for the poor career advice (if any) that you received early on in your life, but from now on your career is in your hands so make a decision to take control.

5 Recognize that your career defines you. People *will* make judgements based on your line of work – what does yours say about you?

6 Dust off your CV and start working on it *now*. Firstly, bring it up to date.

7 Never feel negative about any of the jobs you may have done. They all add experience and prove that you can undertake many things.

8 It is natural at times of change that you will feel depleted in energy and that your mojo has left town, but you don't have to stay like this. Find a source of new energy and get motivated.

9 Start today to look after your body better – think about what, how and when you eat, whether you need any supplements and how you live your life.

10 Look at the training opportunities currently offered by your organization. Is there a programme that you feel would benefit your situation?

Part two

The current situation

Taking stock of now

In this chapter you will learn:
- *how to change your way of thinking*
- *how to bring motivation into work*
- *to present the best image*

In this section we will be looking at your current situation and the opportunities that are open to you right now. Not all opportunities are tangible like training programmes or promotions; many opportunities are revealed through changing your mode of thinking or even your attitude to your current job. For example, an opportunity to rethink your direction might result in deciding to create a different future for yourself. The opportunity here is the space and ability to invest time in rethinking through ideas. After all, there is always more than one way of looking at any situation, and unless we open our minds to other possibilities we will continue to think and do the same things in the same way. So let's start with the inside: our brains, how we use them and how we can make them work for us.

Sorting out the little grey cells

What we think becomes our world. We explored this concept in 'Battling the monster mindset' in Part one of this book where we did an experiment in thinking that today was either going to be a great day or a bad one. If you did this activity you will have been amazed at the power of our brains to create the type of world we expect. Your brain is more than a giant computer; it contains the total world within which you live and work. It is unique to you. No one will think in quite the same way as you and it is this uniqueness that enables others to sometimes see a way out of a situation that we might not have seen ourselves. Furthermore, our brain will work for us in ways we never knew it could *if* we use it effectively.

GETTING CREATIVE

There is a saying, 'If you always do what you've always done, you will always get what you always got' – in other words if we want to find new and different answers to problems we need to change our way of thinking.

Most people agree that throughout the many functions our brain has to orchestrate it tends to work on problems either from an analytical/logical perspective or a creative perspective, and that we tend to have a preference between these that we use more often. It is a bit like a default button on a piece of equipment – you will always default back to your original, more natural way of thinking. This does not mean that we cannot use the other perspective – just that it might not be our first choice. Therefore, stimulating the other perspective is a good place to start when thinking through problems. Let's use the example of your career. You know that you need to change your career but you do not know what you want to do, whether you want to change at all and so forth.

....

If you feel that you need to stimulate your creative perspective	If you feel that you need to stimulate your logical perspective
Create a mood board by sticking images that appeal to you, relating to work (in a similar fashion to creating the wish life collage in Part one).	Think through your hobbies and the type of work you enjoy (such as working with your hands) and list the types of work areas you feel drawn to.
Create an affirmation about the job or outcome you would like and practise it often (see Activity 5).	Plan to visit each of these work areas (or look up details on the internet) and find out the 'real story' about working in these industries.

(Contd)

Find out more about yourself
by undertaking Activity 13
in Part four of this book.

Now plan a step-by-step
procedure for moving
forward, with timeframes
and outcomes.

....

When you stimulate both perspectives of your brain, you create
different ways of looking at problems and issues and therefore you
are more likely to generate a wider number of possible solutions.
Involve more people in helping you and the possibilities become
endless because you are now involving a wider range of perceptions,
assumptions and alternative views. However, through all this
energy, you must remember that at some point you need to make
a decision and act, otherwise all your ideas will have been an
interesting experiment and little else.

Motivation madness

There is no change without motivation. However, the question is
where do you find that motivation? When we are working flat out
it is quite often difficult in the extreme to add other things to our
day. The danger then is that you not only feel like you are treading
water and making no progress but also you begin to get frustrated
from not having the time to progress your dreams. You internalize
your anger at your situation and this can then lead onto the worst
scenario of all – you give up.

Maintaining motivation through any change is difficult. The road
is not necessarily straight and you may find that some routes are
blocked – but you must keep going if you are to succeed. Progress
seems so difficult but going back is not an option. If this sounds
familiar there is an easier way.

FINDING THE TRIGGERS

Let's start with the basics. What motivates you? What makes you
get up in the morning? What do you hope to get out of work? Do
you think about your work in longer terms (such as what you want
to achieve this year) or are you just trying to get through the day?

By identifying some of our basic motivators we can extend these
into our lives and bring richness and enjoyment. Have you ever had

the experience where you come home from work feeling really tired but someone at home had organized a party for you to go to? You don't really want to go but guess what? When you get there you get a sudden surge of energy and find yourself dancing until dawn. We often describe this effect as getting a 'second wind' (similar to the social energy in Part one) – a burst of energy that carries us through, but we only get this sensation when we are enjoying ourselves. Had the party been with people we did not know and was boring, it might just as easily have sent us to bed. We are pleasure seekers and that forms part of our motivation. You can feel energized by a walk out in the sunlight or because someone thanked you for doing a good deed.

Try Activity 14 in Part four of this book. It will show you how to keep a motivation diary that will enable you to identify the types of things that motivate you. To increase your motivation you need to ensure that there are more of these activities factored into your life. For example, if you had a motivation lift when someone brought you a cake back from lunch then you need to first of all separate out whether it was the gesture that was motivational or the treat. If it was the gesture tell the individual how much you appreciated the gesture and it is likely that it will be repeated. If it was the treat itself then plan the odd occasion when you can treat yourself for the work you have done.

BRING ON THE FRIENDS

Friends can be hugely motivational. Tell them what you want to achieve and how you intend getting there – and then ask for their help. If they are true friends they will help you plan and support you on any route that will help you achieve your dreams. Friends can also take you out of yourself. When you feel your motivation sapping they will pick you up and make sure you are pointed back in the right direction.

Often when we embark on a change of career or place of work we might feel we are in danger of compromising those friendships, especially if the career change takes us further away from our friends. However, the world is a much smaller place these days and with social networking and online contact, you are literally only a few clicks away from maintaining those friendships forever.

INTRODUCING A MENTOR

Mentors can help significantly with motivation. Mentors are people who have actually done the job you want to do. They can advise you on the most appropriate course of action, and cut down on the time wasted (and lost) through making mistakes or choosing the wrong option. In essence they have battled their way through the mire before you and have left the path free for you to follow in relatively easier strides.

Mentors can also help you think through areas where you might be flagging. Indecision also saps motivation, and adds delay and frustration – two things we want to avoid as they have such negative outcomes. Mentors can help you set goals (Activity 18 in Part four of this book) and keep upbeat. They can also help you to reframe your thinking (revisit Activity 9 in Part four of this book) so that it is more positive and therefore conducive to producing energy.

WORK NETWORKS

Many occupations have work networks that may be real or virtual. Within a work network you can discuss career aspirations as well as share frustrations. (You might even find out the realities about one of your 'dream' businesses.) You will also be able to do some useful networking and make some friends who all share the same professional interest. Search your area for local meetings or look up various institutes and professional bodies and find out what is happening in your area. You will meet new people and have an outlet for your frustrations.

ACTION LEARNING SETS

Action learning sets are groups where problems are brought to the table and shared. The expected outcome is to find many more possible solutions to the problem – but the actual solution chosen is your choice alone. To gain the greatest variety of solutions action learning sets typically do not comprise people from the same industry or background. If that were the case (such as in the work network example) it is likely that the number of solutions would be smaller and probably very similar to your own. Instead the wide variety of backgrounds creates an even wider variety of possible solutions – even if some of them are decidedly wacky. The great benefit of action learning sets is that you really start to look at the problem from very different perspectives, and that breaks you out of any static thinking.

CREATING SPACE TO THINK AND PLAN

Many people feel that taking time out to think and plan is highly motivational. Do you recall how good you felt when you had had a break or a holiday? The pleasant feeling is not just about seeing blue skies, sand and sea; it is also refreshing to experience some quality time where we can contemplate our lives and think through the next section. That is why so many people set themselves goals and promises while on holiday; it all seems so easy when you have the time. However, quite often when we return reality strikes and we forget all our plans until the next one. That pattern of making promises to yourself and then not acting on them is quite dangerous in terms of motivation. You can seesaw backwards and forwards without actually achieving anything and that will feel uncomfortable. It is relatively easy in this situation to move from 'mover and shaker' one minute to 'under-achiever' the next – and take with it all those feelings of disappointment. To prevent this you need to create a space in your life where you can plan and think, and take your dreams forward in a managed way so that you achieve one or two items before moving on to the next. Don't try to achieve everything at once (see Activity 12 and 18 in Part four of this book) but move forward incrementally, factoring in times for considering your progress. Undertaking a sporting activity is great for this as you are able to think while you run or swim. When you create time for yourself you are also subliminally giving yourself messages that you believe in investing in your thoughts. This will result in higher self-esteem and increased motivation. Book some time in your diary right away!

Looking the part

Our society is incredibly visual. The response to this is to take a good look at ourselves and the image we present. We all know that looks and image are not everything and can be very shallow but still we appraise and make decisions on the way people present themselves. This is because everyone has full control over the way they look and therefore if a person dresses a certain way we assume that they are doing so to reflect an element of their personality.

In other words, they want to promote this look. Reflect for a moment. Who would you like to look like? Is there a person you are modelling yourself on? Do you dress to reflect a certain aspect of your personality? If you are not being taken seriously at work, revitalize your career with a complete image overhaul. It can get you noticed and give you confidence too.

With so many images out there, what do you choose? Revitalizing your career image is not simply wearing what you like – you need to dress appropriately too. Wacky styling is great in an advertising agency where being different is applauded, but not so in a legal firm where you may make clients nervous if you wear your yellow suit with a red shirt or blouse. Clients may feel you are not taking your job seriously and therefore won't be taking their case seriously either. What would be an appropriate style in your working domain?

How we dress then is part of our personality showcase and partly what is appropriate. For this reason we need to ensure our persona promotes our future and relays our expectations to the world. There is no problem with people at the top of their career carving out a unique image for themselves, but if you are looking to move upwards or be accepted into a new area of business you need to dress carefully so that you fit into their mould but with a personal 'twist'. The appropriateness of your style will show that you fit into that 'world' and the twist just adds personality. For example, if you were in the legal profession, you could still wear the regulation deep grey or black suit but add a unique scarf or tie to project a little of your own personality.

DRESS TO BE BEST

Firstly, let's consider the clothes that you wear each day. Naturally if you wear a uniform there is little opportunity to express yourself beyond that as this is the very point of any organization requiring uniformed dress – that everyone looks the same and represents a carefully chosen image. However, many organizations will leave dress up to your own interpretation (usually within certain parameters). Looking good is one of the fastest routes to being noticed for progression, and one way to ensure you look good is to consider these three elements of dress in your current workplace:

▶ The overall dress code
▶ Quality
▶ Expression.

The dress code

Look around you and see how people are clothed. You may be in a very formal environment or an informal one but start to become very aware of who wears what and when. Does your organization have a policy on clothing? If you are unsure find out now and check out the rules. Some of the rules may be set for safety reasons, for example, the wearing of flip flops in the office can be quite dangerous as they leave the foot unsupported and uncovered. Other rules may be for modesty reasons or for company image. Quite often there is a different dress code for those who are dealing with customers from those who provide a back office (or support) function.

Many companies today offer staff a dress-down day once a week (typically a Friday) to boost staff morale and allow personal expression. However, if your company does this does everyone comply? Do managers wear a different mode of dress than other workers? Messages around dress code can be surprisingly subtle and unwritten. For example, your organization may offer a 'dress-down Friday' but do all the managers comply? And if not, is there a secret message going on here?

Finally avoid dressing provocatively. It rarely wins friends and does not present a professional image. If you are not careful you may find that rather than look sensual you just look cheap and capable of poor judgement.

Quality

If you do not already, start to observe the difference in quality of clothing. These days there is no excuse for anyone who is working not to be able to afford one smart item of clothing as it has never been easier to afford quality garments even on a tight budget. The term 'quality' here does not mean 'designer' wear but good, well-made clothes that do not sag or slouch on the body.

This advice is not just about the look but also the feel. When you wear well-made, tailored clothes you will feel so much better and exude a confidence that you do not feel in cheaper items.

If cost is a major issue for you a top tip is to splash out on a sharp jacket with a great cut and style, but in a plain block colour (such as charcoal grey, navy or black). Ladies can then cut back in cost on toning trousers, skirts, blouses and shirts. Just one point for gentlemen here: suit jackets and trousers should always be bought together otherwise they will not match, but you can make economies with shirts and ties. With a dark background you can then afford to alternate the other more colourful garments around this look and still remain very smart. By changing the colour of shirts, tops, blouses, ties and accessories, you will obtain a number of 'looks' from one basic staple. Have your jacket or suit dry-cleaned but make sure the other items can be washed in a regular washing machine, again to keep costs to a manageable level.

Finally invest in a good coat that you will wear for years and matches as much of your workwear as possible. You may think that what you wear in and out of work is not noticed but it is, and a smart coat can set the tone as it covers instantly any clothing under it.

Expression

If everyone dressed in the same way life would be so boring. Thank goodness for accessories that brighten any outfit and make chain store staples look more individual. However, a word of warning – your accessories are an expression of yourself. Whether you choose to wear an understated silk tie or a cartoon character, each one says so much about you, so choose the right image that you want to convey. Fashion, too is very expressive but on occasions it can also be quite aggressive and therefore you need to think carefully about your industry and what it will tolerate or accept.

Also use colour carefully. Some colours work better with different hair and skin colours, while others seem to drain us. Colour can also send powerful messages – there are many organizations that still consider that wearing a red jacket is an aggressive statement. If you are unsure keep bright colours only for accessories and limit your working wardrobe to plain colours.

Insight

Don't dress for who you are now, dress for the person you want to be. This way you will be noticed and it will seem the most natural move in the world to appoint you into your future role as you visually fit in already.

A MENTION ABOUT GENERAL GROOMING

It might seem old-fashioned to consider our general grooming but all the clothes in the world will not convey the right image if you have dirty fingernails, greasy hair or body odour.

Check out that you are presenting yourself in the best possible light and if you are unsure ask an honest friend to advise you.

Another aspect of personal grooming is hairstyle. Again, look at the people who are dressed for where you want to be – what is their hair like? Basically you want a style that reflects your personality and is easy to maintain. If you decide you want to incorporate hair colour then factor in the cost of ongoing maintenance. Maintaining intricate styles and colour combinations can be expensive, so either learn to colour your hair yourself or ensure you can pay for regular salon sessions because root growth looks messy and unappealing. Regular haircuts will not only keep your hairstyle neat but will also inspire you to think in terms of grooming as a continual process.

Finally, don't forget your shoes. Shoes that look worn or severely scratched need replacing *now*. There is no excuse as most towns have a shoe repairer, and repairing a good pair of shoes is still cheaper than buying new ones. It may seem old fashioned but many people still judge candidates by their shoes, so therefore ensure yours are smart and well polished.

WALK TALL

Confidence is an interesting quality. The most amazing thing about it is that even if we lack personal confidence it is fairly easy to persuade others that we are the most confident person in the world. Why would we want to do that, I hear you ask. Well, would you trust your business to someone who is so obviously unsure of their ability? No, of course not, and therefore it makes perfect sense that if we want people to trust us with important projects, and we have little in the way of past experience or solid track record to recommend us, then we need to exude confidence.

Confident people do not slouch, they do not sidle into a room or stand back when with others. Therefore you must not either. Start to walk tall. When you enter a room it should be with presence and if volunteers are asked for, step forward. Look around at your colleagues and any impressive managers. Choose someone whose body language conveys just the right amount of confidence you would feel content with, and then observe how they move and how and where they sit. Do not choose someone who is brash and over-confident, aim for a more discreet confidence that exudes trust. Notice how they operate and start to model your body language on theirs. What starts off as an experiment will soon become the way you naturally move and interact, and I can guarantee you will begin to feel more confident as a result.

MOVING AROUND

How do you move around the workplace? Do you sit with good posture and rise elegantly – or dash about haphazardly? Smooth movements convey confidence and assurance, someone in charge of the situation, whereas fast and furious movements can make you appear disorganized.

Start to become very aware of how you:

- ▶ move from one place to another
- ▶ sit and stand
- ▶ answer the telephone
- ▶ move around the workplace
- ▶ go through doors.

If you are unsure of your movements, ask a friend to video you – you may be amazed at the results!

Consider your manners – do you hold doors open for others? Let others go first? Be helpful and considerate? Thank others for their help? Become observant of those in the job position you covet, and adapt your image accordingly. Start the metamorphosis into the person you want to be.

For a fast checklist of the areas you need to consider, see Activity 15 in Part four of this book.

4

....

Developing your skills

In this chapter you will learn:
- *the importance of looking into the future*
- *some suggested key skills to consider*
- *questions you should be asking yourself and others*

We have already looked at your current skills but we also need to look at the skills that are worth developing for the future, to make sure that you are prepared. Twenty years ago, organizations were looking for staff that could use certain software packages (or anyone who was not afraid of a computer!). Today computerization has taken over and become positively mainstream. I remember, in 1990, being told by a friend that I was 'clever' for being able to use a computer. I don't think that skill would justify me being 'clever' by today's standards. Not only have computers entered most areas of work but now, as professionals, we need to consider whether computerization can replicate or even improve our working practices.

If this is to be our future, what additional skills are left for people to gain or hone? Use Activity 16 in Part four of this book to help with your predictions.

Crystal ball gazing – skills for the future

Futurologists predict a workplace where, although all the mundane jobs are automated, it is still staffed by the human race. Therefore the future skills required will be focused on dealing with colleagues, motivating other people, having a customer focus, influencing and negotiating, in addition to practical skills such as running a budget and project management. Although this is not a definitive list it is sufficient to get us started, so let's look at these in more detail.

DEALING WITH COLLEAGUES

Even if you are a whizz at work on your own, beavering away on your own projects, at some point you will need to work with colleagues. This may be in a permanent team situation or simply on an 'as and when' basis. Everyone has their own agenda and so this can sometimes be tricky. In addition, there are a lot of difficult people around and to get ahead you need to be able to demonstrate how you are able to handle difficult personalities and diffuse people problems, as well as work within a team.

The role of team member (or leader) has become increasingly important in recent years, and there appears to be no change to this trend in the future. Even lone workers are usually grouped into one team or another, as being in a team has been demonstrated to increase the worker's feeling of wellbeing. Through being in a team, you are actively contributing towards outcomes bigger and further reaching than you would have achieved alone.

Questions to ask yourself	Questions to ask others
How experienced are you in working in (or leading) a team?	How do I interact well with everyone in the team?
How are my person management skills?	How well do you think I deal with team and personal issues?
Do I need to read more about dealing with difficult people?	Am I happy to take feedback from the team/colleagues?

MOTIVATING OTHERS

Being able to motivate others is the key to getting things done. You will not be able to achieve everything that you want to achieve on your own, and therefore getting other people 'on board' and willing to work and support your goals is a key skill.

Motivating others is not about false platitudes, it is about creating an atmosphere that is dynamic and enjoyable for the team, so that they are able to work more effectively. In some instances it includes introducing new ideas (for example, frothy coffee on Friday), and in other instances it includes ruling out unpopular bureaucracy such as getting rid of petty rules that serve no purpose.

Questions to ask yourself	Questions to ask others
How can I increase the motivation for others in the team?	What motivates you?
What do I need to learn about motivation?	Do you find me motivating?
What small measures can I introduce to create a more motivating atmosphere?	How can I develop to be a more motivating colleague/leader?

HAVING A CUSTOMER FOCUS

I mentioned earlier in this section how it used to be possible to select staff based on their computer knowledge, whereas today most people are quite accomplished computer operators. Now and in the future you are more likely to be tested on your attitude and the level of customer focus you have. The reasoning behind this is that you can be taught computer (or any operative) skills, but if you do not come to the workplace with the right attitude it is unlikely that going on a training course will help you. In addition it is now recognized that we are all customers of each other, internal and external to the organization, and that we should be treating each other as such.

Customer focus and a need to provide a good service are what make the difference between a good company and a great one. Good customer focus also has the payback of increasing job satisfaction for staff.

Questions to ask yourself	Questions to ask others
How can I introduce or implement more measures of customer care into my job?	To what extent do you feel I incorporate customer care in my work?
Do I truly practise customer care even with internal staff and those in other departments?	What other aspects of customer care could I introduce?

(Contd...)

Questions to ask yourself	Questions to ask others
If I had to evidence my customer care approach to another employer, how would I do that?	Do I differentiate between external and internal customers?

BEING INFLUENTIAL

We all know of some teams that we would love to be in, and some managers we would love to work for. It is often difficult to pinpoint the one reason for this. Call it charisma or presence, some people just beg to be listened to and make popular managers. What we are really describing here is a form of influence. People who are influential make things happen. They mix with the right people and pick up the plum projects – on which of course they succeed because they have so many colleagues wanting to help them.

Being influential is not all about what you know but it does include a large dose of quiet confidence and self-assurance, both of which may need to be developed.

Questions to ask yourself	Questions to ask others
Who do I feel is influential at work?	Do you believe I am influential in any part of my work?
What makes them so?	What do you believe creates influence?
If I could replicate that quality, would I have the same level of influence?	If you were me, where do you think I could extend my range of influence?

POLITICAL AWARENESS

Being politically aware means knowing who the movers and shakers at work are and how they operate. All organizations are structured like small countries with rulers, influential people and characters who have certain amounts of power. Being able to read the signals and anticipate actions and events is the essence of political awareness. If you find yourself saying, 'How come I did not see that coming?' you need to work on your political awareness.

Questions to ask yourself	Questions to ask others
Who are the movers and shakers in this company?	What do you need to do to make things happen here?
How do those in power hold onto and exercise that power?	How political do you think you need to be around here?
What 'other games' are being played out here?	What are the indications of a large change happening around here?

NEGOTIATING A GOOD DEAL

As we have seen, in the future excellent communication skills will be essential, and those that succeed will be the people who know how to work closely and productively with others – and this includes striking deals that benefit both parties. Whether you are asking for an increased salary or allocating work to others, the ability to negotiate should be high on your agenda of key skills.

In the past it may have been acceptable to strike forth for the deal you wanted and pay little concern to the outcome for the other party. This is no longer the case. In all likelihood you will be working with this person again in the future and a more equitable outcome for both of you will ensure that you return to the business table, respecting each other. The emphasis then is on long-term relationships, rather than short-term quick wins.

Questions to ask yourself	Questions to ask others
Where, with whom, and in what situations do I negotiate?	How forceful is my negotiating style?
Do I always consider what would be a good outcome for the other party too?	Would you describe negotiation as a strength of mine?
Do I need to attend a training programme to help with my negotiating skills?	How could my negotiating skills be improved?

Until now we have been considering soft skills – the ones you employ when working with others. However, not all skills on my list for the future are soft ones. The following two are technical skills that I believe will be very important.

BUDGETING

All work runs to a budget. Your organization or workplace has to cover the cost of employing you, including paying for your workspace and any benefits you may enjoy. Having a knowledge of the business you work in, and how the profits are made (and spent), are the top level aspect of budgeting. At a more local level is the ability to run a budget for your team, department or unit. Financial acumen is a very desirable skill because a business cannot run without it, and it is fundamental to the role of manager. So, if you are unsure of figures, dust off your ego and take advantage of one of the many courses available today that enable you to gain a qualification in finance.

Questions to ask yourself	Questions to ask others
How comfortable do I feel about budgeting and figure work?	Where does the company publish its profits and losses?
Do I really understand how the finances are generated and spent in my workplace/ organization?	Who deals with the budgets for our team (and can I see them)?
Do I need to improve my skills in this area?	Can I go on a budgeting/finance course please?

PROJECT MANAGEMENT

The second of my technical skills is project management. Most pieces of work are now called 'projects' and the more you move upwards in your career the more you will be required not only to run projects but also oversee other projects, and that includes understanding project reports. Not all projects are of the size and significance to require you to use the full range of project management tools, but a familiarity with them enables you to take from the discipline those that you feel would be helpful.

Project management is seen as a skill in itself and therefore is a welcome addition to your CV.

Questions to ask yourself	Questions to ask others
Does any of my current work fall under the definition of a project?	Is anyone else working under the project management discipline and can I speak to them?
Do I envisage a need for project management skills in the future?	What aspects of project management could help my present job?
Am I the sort of person who likes to be organized?	Does the organization have any books on project management that I could read?

5

Opportunities are all around

In this chapter you will learn:
- *the value of opportunities*
- *how to find opportunities*
- *how to make contacts*

Opportunities are all around us but quite often we do not see them because we are not looking in the right places. Have you ever been in the situation of being a passenger in a car after many years of being the driver? If so, you will have noticed all kinds of buildings that you never noticed as a driver because when you were driving your focus was always on the road and you were concentrating on manoeuvres, rather than the scenery. This phenomenon is replicated in the workplace. You do not always see the opportunities around you because you are too focused on your job and the way you feel about your job to see beyond its parameters.

Look around you – what do you see?

If you have been undertaking the activities in Part four of this book, you will have found out some interesting things about yourself and what you like, and you may even know where you want to go from here. This can provide you with a very forward-looking focus, which is great – after all, you want to get up and started, don't you? However, what you may be unaware of, is that the start of your journey could be right under your nose, in the organization, business or company in which you already work. Do not be too quick to leap off and into a new job. Be patient and wait until you have learned as much as you can from the workplace you are currently in.

WORK PROJECTS

Who decides which person undertakes the latest projects? Why don't you volunteer to undertake one of those projects? Even if it is a stretch, you could learn so much and of course these skills are ones that you will take to whichever job you have from here onwards. It would certainly be safe testing ground for you to experiment and see where your talents lie and whether you like specific aspects of that job. (If you find that you have a flare for project management then perhaps you should become a professional project manager.)

PEOPLE

What type of people work in your industry? Do they have to fit a mould or are they quite eclectic? Are there distinct layers of hierarchy in your company and do they attract specific types of people in each layer? Who are the real influencers?

You may not have paid much attention to the people at work, other than work colleagues, but from now on I want you to give them your full attention. There is a truism I want to share with you:

People recruit people. What I mean by this is that no matter how long your list of qualifications and skills if the person responsible for deciding whether to employ you doesn't like you then they will not employ you. It does not sound fair or right but unfortunately life's like that.

The relationships you make at work and the impression you give will always give you the first 'foot in the door' and also the 'final say' (the middle section is slightly more flexible!). That is why internal candidates quite often fare better than external ones.

The other point to note is that the people you work with all have other contacts such as family members and friends, and therefore the key to your future career might be just a conversation away. Refer to Activity 19 'Networking' in Part four of this book. We will be using it fully later, but you might like to start thinking of the contacts you work with and who may be very helpful indeed.

SKILLS

We have looked at skills for the future in a previous section, but I really want you to think about what skills are being offered around you now. Have you looked in your training brochure or have you questioned what courses you could go on? Perhaps you sit next to someone who manages the budget and you could ask them to show you how that side of the business works. After all, you never know when someone might be off sick and the position needs cover. There should always be some form of multi-tasking in organizations as it is useful for people to be able to cover each other's jobs in an emergency, and if it is not in place perhaps you could suggest it. You would learn more skills and the business would gain from lowering the risk of being without a key person at a very busy time.

CREATING OPENINGS

Does your organization liaise with, or support, a charity? Perhaps you could suggest it, if it doesn't. If it does already, what does it do and is there anything more that could be done? What we are doing here is creating openings for interesting projects and areas where you can develop a lead role. Many companies are now engaging in community projects such as going into partnership with a school, and these offer a plethora of development opportunities. They are also interesting and can be fun, but don't wait to be invited – help create the opening first.

PERKS

What are the great things that your current job brings? When we ache to move jobs we forget all the good things that were available in our current job – we talk ourselves into thinking that the other job offers so much more, don't we?

We forget that extra day of leave every month, working so near home that we don't need to maintain a car, the pension plan or the fact that you get free tea and coffee. Whatever is on offer at your business, make a list now of all the good things your current job offers. Think in terms of freebies (those beverages), any discount deals, leave, working hours, uniforms, insurance and pensions, financial deals, Christmas presents (gifts and meals), travel supplements, sick pay, bonuses, free computing, flexible hours, the Christmas party, prizes and so forth. Your job is not just the day job – it is for this reason that personnel officers will always speak in terms of an employment 'package'. Consider the package you are offered, and revel in some of the incentives. If they are not available in your dream job, consider how you would reconcile that. As a way of capturing this information, look at Activity 17 in Part four of this book.

Work projects, people and skills are around you now, but you will never notice them until you lose your tunnel vision and start noticing the opportunities in front of you.

Who and what do you actually work for?

Time to delve deeper into the opportunities that surround you. People take jobs for many reasons: sometimes it is to join a particular industry or sector, because of the organizational values, or it might be the job itself, the location, or for some people it is simply because it is a job when they are currently unemployed. Whatever your reasons for ending up in your current employment, it pays to take a deeper look at the organization and all that it stands for. You may find that your employer is not the organization you thought it was, that your organization has hidden depths – and who knows, you might just fall in love with it all over again.

VALUES

Your organization will have set values that it will promote through its work practices. For example, if you work for an ethical organization, those values should not just be headings on a piece of paper; they should be integrated into every working practice. In essence every employee needs to embody those ethics, and that can be more difficult in a larger organization where there are more layers of management between staff and management. Staying true to organizational ethics is a challenge because organizations change too. What might be easy for a small company to accomplish with perhaps a dozen employees becomes much harder when there are over 100 employees (finding five or six like-minded friends to work together is a cinch but as the numbers grow it is difficult to hang on to those high values, and to expect others to share them). Take that to over 1,000 employees and the challenge becomes even greater.

Some organizations also become confused as they grow. To purport to be an organization that believes in saving the planet and then does not recycle paper or leaves all the lights on after hours is, on the face of it, ridiculous. Most people would agree that this would be hypocritical in the extreme, but organizations are made up of people and if the staff have no interest in the ethics, or do not buy into the businesses' values, their actions can work against the values of the company.

Think back to when you started work in your company. Ask yourself:

- ▶ Did you really understand the implications of the business you were entering and how that converted into actions?
- ▶ Is your current business one which has strong values?
- ▶ Are these values the ones you wish to align yourself with?
- ▶ How do they affect you?

CULTURE

Your company will have a certain culture. Culture simply means 'the way things are done around here'. It can cover every aspect of working life from how decisions are made to who buys the milk for the tea! Culture can be hard to break because it is about habitual behaviour. Unlike values, culture is not written down in a statement and most of it is about practice – but it must not be ignored. If you are a quiet person but the culture of the organization is very dynamic, it may be that you do not feel comfortable and you are often overlooked or perceived as weak. Similarly if you are a highly extroverted egocentric you probably won't fit too well in a library!

Make a note of the cultural elements at play in your workplace and register how you feel about them. Do they matter or do you find them limiting or frustrating?

WHERE IS THE POWER?

It is always useful to know who the influential people are in your workplace. Are they the managers, or do key workers appear to be more powerful? Are all decisions made by one person or is there a panel? Who appoints new staff (human resources may think they do this function but is the decision really down to someone else)?

Identifying the power base can help you to target your enquiries regarding future job opportunities. In some organizations managers are able to appoint staff themselves without more senior jurisdiction. This means that if you were applying to an organization like that you would be better targeting managers than the human resources department.

Power is not all about seniority either. Some people are powerful in their own right and they might be on the same level as you or working in another team. They are usually very aware of their influence and like to demonstrate to others how they can assert their power. You need to identify these people because although they can appear scary at first they can also help you considerably. One word from them and you can be literally included or excluded from a project – therefore these people can be useful friends but difficult enemies.

THE ANNUAL REPORT AND BUSINESS PLAN

I have been asking you to analyse your present company under two headings: firstly to find out who you are currently working for and whether they fit with your view of the world (values and culture), and secondly to identify the power bases. If you are going to make real changes to your working life you need to know what you are dealing with and what to look for in the future. Some of these points require your observation, and others may be found in either your organization's annual report or business plan.

Insight

Your choice of career speaks volumes about you; for example, you would expect the person entering a career in social care to be passionate about this subject, wouldn't you? What does your job say about you and what would you *like* it to say about you?

Learning to love contacts

In an earlier section I mentioned that people recruit, recommend and select other people. In other words, having great qualifications and a stunning CV is only part of the picture – there is still the human element. If you have ever lost out to an internal candidate you will see this behaviour in action and feel that it is grossly unfair. Unfortunately it is all too common and because of this we need it to work in our favour rather than against us.

BEHAVIOUR AND ANIMALS

Humans are animals. We like to feel comfortable with other human beings and therefore a familiar face will always be more welcome than a stranger's. You can see this behaviour in action at weddings and other similar gatherings where a large number of people who do not know each other are thrown together simply because they know the bride and groom. They naturally gravitate towards people they have met before, or try to find any common ground ('Where are you from? Devon? Great, I've been there!')

and when they find commonality they form small subsets. It also happens at conferences where we actively seek out anyone we have met previously, perhaps at another conference, or a work colleague. On training courses, where work colleagues often attend in pairs, they appear to be glued together all day and only feel comfortable in their own group.

As comfortable as this behaviour is, we need to break it otherwise we will not be able to create the kind of contact list that we need. You need to move away from the groups of people you know and introduce yourself to others. Everyone you meet is a possible contact for the future and therefore needs your full attention. Although you should never shun others (especially work colleagues) it is new contacts and connections you need to be fostering, while people you already know become maintenance contacts. They are still important but the effort needed to maintain a contact is less than is needed to create a new one.

LET'S GET STARTED

Activity 19 in Part four of this book includes an exercise for identifying our current network of contacts. You might be surprised at just how many people you know and can legitimately call a contact. Let me surprise you further. All of the people you have listed know other people too. This means that your network is even wider than you thought. If you have a network of 50 people on your list it is highly likely that each of these people also have a network of 50 people – that is a total network of 2,500 contacts you now have access to! How do you reach this extended list? Easy, go through your first contact. If you are professional rather than needy, and are willing to help others reach their aspirations too, it should not be too difficult to ask a favour, such as an introduction to someone else. For example, a contact of mine knows a director working in TV. I could say to my contact, 'I would like to ask you a favour. I am thinking of changing my career and I am interested in working in television. I know you have a colleague in this field and I wondered whether you could ask them if it would be possible to either buy them a coffee or have a short telephone conversation, so that I can ask a couple of questions. I don't know anyone else in that industry and your help would be invaluable.' How could you refuse such a request?

It is said that there are only six degrees of separation between ourselves and the thing we want to find or locate. Be persistent – the person who holds the key to your door is out there, but you might need to speak to a lot of people first. Enjoy the process; so many people enjoy talking about their own work and giving an insight to others that they are generally very flattered when another person finds them (or what they do) interesting. This means that on most occasions they are more than happy to give advice or direct you on to another colleague – it is just that we never feel able to ask. Social media has helped considerably in this area. You may find that you can extend your network of contacts via this mechanism too.

If you have a refusal simply thank them for coming back to you, and then reroute your search in a different direction. Never pester or abuse a contact – you need to respect everyone's time and energy limits. It may be that through handling a refusal correctly you are able to win this person over and they offer you another date and time to talk that is less pressured.

GETTING ORGANIZED

Now that you have seen the value of networking and tracking a list of contacts, you need to organize yourself effectively.

▶ Introducing yourself – We covered this earlier. You need to create an interesting introduction for yourself, and Activity 7 ('Meet and greet people with impact') in Part four of this book will help you create just that.

▶ Business cards – By far the easiest way of maintaining a list of business contacts is by collecting their business cards. This means that you also need a business card to give back. If your company does not provide business cards personal ones can be bought very cheaply online. There is no issue with you having your own business card as long as it states only your name and your personal contact details. This means not having the company logo on it or your job title.

▶ Storage – When someone gives you their business card and the conversation has finished, take out a pen or pencil and note on the back of the card the date and where you met (and any key words that will help you remember the person, such as what you were discussing). This is a useful habit to get into because there could be quite a few cards coming your way during a conference. When you get home and empty your case, you need to know who was which contact, and which ones should be followed up. Another way to store contacts is to either get a manual filing system with cards that you can glue the business card to and then write details around it, or to transfer it to your electronic organizer for safekeeping.

▶ Contacts list – You might also want to create a contacts list in a database format so that you are able to select, for example, all your contacts who are in the printing business. This method would enable you to send out certain information to a discrete list of contacts and not to everyone. This searching ability would take a long time if you were trying to do it by hand, but using a database makes this easy.

▶ Keeping in touch – Now that you have this list you really should be using it to stay in touch. In marketing this is called keeping your contacts 'warm'. Start by sending them an email or note saying how good it was to meet them and how you will maintain their details for the future. From then onwards aim to send some message to them at least quarterly to maintain contact. Also consider business networking sites such as LinkedIn. It is simple to create an account and you may find you are automatically linked with other professionals.

Reaching outside the company

So far we have limited our contact list to people we know and their colleagues. Now we need to go further afield. There is a whole big world outside your present employment, full of people who really want to help you.

We don't always feel it appropriate to knock on other people's doors for information but it is much easier than you may think if you are genuine. Many years ago I was researching for a Masters qualification and needed certain information from large 'blue chip' organizations. My first thought was that none of these organizations would speak to little old me. After all, who was I? Just some student who was asking questions! What would they get out of speaking to me? How wrong can you be?

I wrote to all of them and was most surprised not only to receive replies but also, in two cases, to be invited in to discuss how they could help me. I will repeat that – *how they could help me*. I was overawed by their generosity and one of them actually invited me to sit in on one of their training programmes, a place that my employer at that time could not have afforded for me to go on. When I thanked them they told me that they love to help but that they rarely get requests. This may not be the experience every time but it shows that there are generous organizations out there that are only too happy to share their knowledge and expertise, if you just ask.

FINDING WHAT YOU WANT

Initially you need to be clear as to why you are reaching out to other organizations. For example, are you networking in general or are you trying to find out specific information? Are you seeking information *about how to get into* a certain career (facts) or are you *trying to get a feel* for working in that sector (experiencing emotions) to see if it is for you?

If you know whom you want to contact then fine but if not you will need to do some research so that you locate the right organization to give you the information or experience you need. You can look:

▶ locally – Your local library will have a list of all major businesses in your locality, but apart from addresses they will not give out contact details.
▶ regionally – Your local Chamber of Commerce will have a list of members, including contact details of many organizations, but note that this will not be everyone in the region, only those businesses who are members. However, the contact information will be quite detailed and Chamber members are largely open to helping others.
▶ nationally and internationally – Search the internet for organizational headquarters and then ring to make contact. Do not worry about speaking to a receptionist – they know everyone in the organization and will hopefully be able to route your enquiry in the right direction.

Make your first objective to meet the person concerned as soon as possible. It may be for just a cup of coffee but once you have met someone there is a bond between you, and from there you can progress to ask whatever you want, perhaps for more data or for detailed information on how to get a specific job there. This has the added bonus in that you can also always go back to them in the future with the 'I'm sure you recall that we met last year to discuss ...' line. Very few people would say, 'No, I don't remember' to this, even if they genuinely don't remember because that may make them appear foolish. They are more likely to say, 'Ah yes' in a vague way and while they are thinking wildly, trying to place you, you are in an excellent position to state your request.

Finally, follow up with a thank you note. Yes, I am sure you thanked them on the day but a handwritten note is very personal and always admired – and of course, add them to your contacts list. Even if you never contact them again, you may need their details for a friend.

6

....

Appreciating the day to day

In this chapter you will learn:
- *how to make the most of your day*
- *to re-name days to bring fun into work*
- *the importance of rewards*

This section of the book is about your current situation, and as mentioned earlier, there may be many reasons why you might not be in a position to move to another job at the moment. It could be because of:

▶ the economic situation
▶ the fact that your current employer is just so great you don't want to leave them
▶ the team is fantastic
▶ you enjoy your job
▶ the workplace is situated in the ideal location
▶ the hours fit in with caring responsibilities ...

... and so forth. Whatever the reason, for some people staying put just seems the right choice for now. However, that does not mean you have to grin and bear it. Earlier in the book we explored ways of changing our mindset and becoming more motivated in work. This was because the more enjoyment we find in our work, the more satisfied we will be, and our wellbeing will increase exponentially. So how do we create fun in the workplace and gain the benefit, without being thought foolish or silly?

Having a great day

Every day can be a great day if we want it to be (and we explored how in 'Battling the monster mindset in Part one). However, just thinking it so is only part of the picture – we need to add in some motivators to keep us going throughout the day.

Before we start, a word of warning! Fun activities do not go down well in every workplace and therefore they must be tempered to fit your own organizational culture. Wearing a clown suit into a solicitor's office might not go down well, and would be more likely to get you the sack than any promotion. I am therefore suggesting a gentler version of fun and I will leave it up to you to scale it up or down to fit your workplace. Here are just a couple of suggestions:

THEME OR TREAT OF THE DAY

If you have five people in the workplace, ask each one to create a theme or provide a treat for the day. For example, Monday could be chocolate cake day, Tuesday could be cappuccino day, and so forth all the way through the week.

RE-NAME THE DAY

Fit an activity to the name of the day, for example 'Thank you Thursday' when everyone needs to be super aware of thanking all other staff for their work and interactions with them.

LET'S REMIND OURSELVES

Every job has tedious moments and inspirational ones, but it is easy to slip into thinking our job is the pits and that it offers us little more than employment. Earlier in Part two I asked you to list the perks of your job. I now want you to copy that list into your diary and read it every day while thinking, 'How lucky I am to have a job with all these benefits.' Every time you think your job is just a paying job, read through the list and remind yourself of the benefits on offer to you.

LEARN-SOMETHING-NEW DAY

Ask everyone (perhaps once a month) to teach someone in the team (or the whole team) something new during lunchtime. It might be a smattering of Italian or how to make a gateau; how to knit or how to put up a picture perfectly; how to make a bath bombe gift or how to change a tyre. You will be learning new skills at the same time as working, and it might even become one of the benefits of working there (as mentioned in the previous paragraph). Just think what you could learn in one year.

All these ideas are suggestions for bringing innocent frivolity and gratitude into work. Stay away from more questionable areas such as betting or gambling if at all possible.

Rewarding yourself for getting this far

This section of the book looks at where you are in your current work and suggests different ways you could view your current situation. It builds on your earlier, exploratory work but also aims to enable you to think clearly about the opportunities that surround you. We so often do not see the opportunities for growth and career enjoyment that are under our noses. Nostalgia can also be an interesting phenomenon. When I speak to people in relation to career coaching they often reminisce about previous jobs, saying that they wish they had never left the very companies that, at the time, they were screaming to get away from. It is such a shame that they had to leave to see the organization's good points. If they had thought through the implications of their actions *before* leaving they might never have left and would have saved themselves a lot of difficulty. That is not to say that you should not move on, but you need to do so with the clear understanding of what you are leaving behind and what 'Holy Grail' you hope to find in your new job that appears not to be present in this one.

If you have been undertaking all the activities in Part four of this book, you will have reached a balanced understanding of yourself, your skills and your situation, and from here we will move on to how you can start to build a stronger profile and look to the future. However, before we do that it is time to be rewarded for getting this far. Self-analysis is far from easy – after all, we do not always like the things we find out about ourselves, and sometimes we are our own worst critic, but it is time to brush that aside and revel in some reward for your work so far.

Rewarding yourself is something you should get used to. It is highly motivating and reminds us that we have brought a piece of work or a part of the business to fruition. In essence it is symbolic of closure as well as an opportunity to celebrate the completion of a project. However, how we reward ourselves is important. Here are some guidelines to inspire you:

▶ Rewards are meant to be treats – They are not supposed to be things that you usually do. If you always have chocolate biscuits with your tea, then even an additional one will not really seem much of a reward. However, if you never touch chocolate biscuits but love them, one might be a suitable reward.

▶ Rewards should represent the size of the task – A chocolate biscuit as a reward for writing a book would not seem much of a reward, but for finishing off that pile of filing it might be considered as being just right. The novelist Jacqueline Wilson buys herself a ring every time one of her books is published – now that is more of a reward!

▶ Rewards are satisfiers but can also be motivators – You are rewarding yourself for getting to a certain point in your work, life or career, but could the reward also be a motivator? Imagine, as Jacqueline Wilson was selecting her ring she saw another she liked, would that motivate her to get back home and start on the next book so that she could buy that ring too?

▶ Rewards should be guilt free – If you have done the work or a task then you should be rewarded for it – guilt free. This means that a chocolate biscuit is not the right reward if, after eating it, you then regret the calories. If this strikes home with you use a different reward instead.

▶ Rewards need to become a regular feature of your life – When you reward yourself you feel good. If the reward is right then you also start looking for other projects that can offer a similar reward – and therefore you achieve so much more than others. Get used to rewarding yourself – it pays back in more than one way, and you might find that you like it!

Case studies

CAROL

Carol is starting to recognize that she is capable of so much more if she would like to extend herself within Morgan Pilchard, and that she does not have to move to get more responsibility and expertise.

She likes the organization and the other staff; she is just a little bored because there are few challenges.

Carol has recognized that she does not really know much about the company and what other development opportunities it offers. The senior partners are open to most ideas and Carol starts to think of skills she might need in the future. She starts to wonder whether there are any courses she could go on to become more like a senior in the business and she searches online and enquires at her local college and Adult Education establishment. She also asks Mr Morgan whether she can organize for the monthly local institute meeting to be held in Morgan Pilchard offices so that she can be present. Perhaps then she can make more contacts and begin to ask them how they got into the business.

SAMIA

Samia realizes that she does not really know anything about the factory. She asks for literature on the company and finds out that the re-organization being experienced in her unit is to allow another new unit to be formed to deal with the new project. Her mind starts to race ahead and she wonders whether there will be new jobs created in the other section. They may need an estimator there, or perhaps someone who can handle a project. By thinking through her skills, Samia has recognized that her finance skills are actually very useful in many different careers. She has read up on project management and it seems to her that she would be able to deal with many of the situations that appear to come under that heading.

Samia is also very fashion conscious and starts to think that perhaps some of her work outfits are not as professional as some of the other managers. True, she is not a manager yet, but would anyone consider her to be in the running for a job like that in her present attire? She starts to look at the type of clothes worn by the female managers and goes home to sort out her wardrobe.

JASON

Jason is starting to address some of his behaviour; he has also made an appointment with HR to talk through his situation. He wants to find out what training is on offer for someone like himself. For the first time he is appreciating that working on the factory floor can be a plus because it gives him an insight into how the products are made and how to get along with the workforce. If he were to be promoted this experience would be invaluable. He wants to know whether there are opportunities for him to become a supervisor with a view to becoming a floor manager. He realizes that he will need training but again he needs to find out what is available through work before he starts looking outside (he has already found out that his local Adult Education programme offers management programmes at evening school). This would enable him to continue work and still improve himself. He has heard on the grapevine that the factory has just won a large contract. If that is true then there could be good opportunities in the future because they will need more factory lines and people to supervize and manage them. How can he find out for certain? Perhaps he could try making some contacts.

HENRI

Henri goes through very detailed household accounts with Sarah to ascertain how much he needs to make in the future. There are the university fees to consider and they still want a holiday once a year. When they reach a figure, it is lower than Henri expected (mainly because he still has his redundancy pay). Henri now starts to consider other options that are totally different to any he has thought through before. Henri learned to play the clarinet several years ago. He only plays as a hobby but starts to think that he could form a group or play with a band. He could even go around visiting care homes and play for the people there, as many homes have an entertainment budget. Henri also has a passion for ships and photography, and he is thinking of combining those two together to provide talks on cruise liners. He could design a number of short talks and use his photographs as illustrations. He and Sarah would also benefit from a free holiday, which would mean a reduction in household expenditure. Suddenly some very exciting avenues have opened up and Henri needs to make some firm decisions. He uses the action plan once again, and is starting to plan a way forward.

CHRIS

Chris undertakes the activity 'Who do I think I am?' and it forces her to realize that, although she liked working in the estate agency, there were some aspects that she did not like. This helped her move on to what she really likes and she fills a sheet of paper with all the things she likes in life. One thing that keeps popping up over and over again is the thought of working somewhere where she makes a real difference, possibly with families and very young children. She remembered something that her mother said to her many years ago about how she always thought Chris would work in the medical profession, because she had a pleasant manner and was good with people. Chris starts to put all this together and wonders what is out there that draws these factors together. She decides to visit the Job Centre and ask if they have a career adviser to help her. Her experience with the estate agency has scared her a little and she decides that although you can never be certain about a job moving away from you, surely some jobs are always in demand.

10 THINGS TO REMEMBER

1 When you come across a setback or something you don't like but cannot control, experiment with changing your thinking. This does not mean accepting the situation but seeing whether there is a different way to look at the challenge, and asking yourself why it pushes so many 'hot buttons' for you. It won't help you turn the tide but it might help you ride the waves.

2 Work in accordance with your own motivational triggers. Emotionally, people can go from despair to exhilaration within minutes, thereby demonstrating the volcanic eruptions that make up our psyche. Learn how motivation can drive us and how our motivation is not at the behest of others – we can create our own motivation very efficiently.

3 Never underestimate the power of how you present yourself. We live in a highly visual world – a world that also makes snap judgements based on looks, carriage and style. There are many unwritten rules as to how to behave in business and at work – take time to learn them.

4 Gathering skills for today will result in you being highly skilled for work now and, importantly, developing skills for tomorrow. Look at where your chosen profession has come from, and try to find out where it is going in the future. There will be more technology and a greater need for people skills in addition to literacy and numeracy skills.

5 Recognize the true worth of your present business. It always seems like someone else has the better deal, but is that really true? What do you value in work and does a slightly higher pay packet compensate for losing that?

6 Engage in your business to a greater degree. Does your company support any charities? Are there aspects of your company that you do not know? How healthy are its profits and are there opportunities for expansion? If you see an opportunity on the horizon, could you approach someone about being involved first?

7 Look on everyone as a possible contact for the future. Actively ask them about their friends, relations, and contacts – try to build a network for your future business. People love to help other people, so keep a file of business cards and have some made yourself.

8 Think outside of your company – future contacts are everywhere. Take any opportunity to go to trade fairs or to visit other businesses. You never know whom you might meet or the jobs that may be available in the future.

9 Make every day a fantastic day. Actively bring enjoyment into the workplace. Be the first to introduce something wacky and different. Life is what you make it, so make it good.

10 If you have been undertaking the activities so far – give yourself a reward. Perhaps buy another book or treat yourself to lunch out. You deserve it for all your hard work ... now onto the next part!

Part three
Looking to the future

7

Getting ready for success

In this chapter you will learn:
- *how to prepare mentally*
- *how to prepare physically*
- *the importance of building resilience*

Preparing for the future can be exciting and invigorating. The world is your oyster, and there are as many opportunities available as you have ideas. The temptation to rush forward with these ideas is very strong indeed, but wait, hold back a little longer. Before we can forge ahead we really need to create some firm foundations to build on, and that means starting with the mind and body.

Balancing the mind and body

THE RIGHT ATTITUDE

Whether we are looking for a totally new direction or to reignite interest in our current job, we need to ensure we have the right attitude. That attitude comes from having energy that is focused on making progress towards our goals (see Activity 18 in Part four of this book). Being focused not only targets our thought processes and talents but also increases the chances of us attaining those goals. For example, you are interviewing two candidates and you have asked each why they want to work for this company:

Person A: I have wanted to work at Bilchards for over four years now. I have followed your growth from small company into market leader with interest, and have always felt that I wanted to be part of a winning team. I read recently that you plan to extend into Europe with your product, something that I find very exciting.

Person B: I want to work for Bilchards because you are the largest employer in the area, and I don't really want to travel. I need to tell you though, I have also applied for jobs at Hughes and Skimore's too.

Which one would you choose? Would it be the person with the passion, or the one that takes a 'scattergun' approach to job seeking? If they were the same in every other way, I would hope that you would give serious consideration to selecting the person who impressed you with their enthusiasm and highly focused thinking, rather than a candidate who thought your job was no more attractive than any other, whatever their interview technique.

We can teach so many skills, but we cannot change people's attitudes – they have to do that themselves. If a new candidate is employed with the wrong attitude, it is highly unlikely that they will change. What is worse is that this attitude can spread to others, breeding negativity and suspicion. I am sure you would not want to bring that into your team, and therefore ensuring you have the right attitude towards any future job prospects can literally be the key to the job – and so:

▶ get your thinking right
▶ whether changing or staying, feel content that this is the job for you at this moment in time
▶ don't be afraid to show your enthusiasm – it could clinch the deal.

VISUALIZATION

Visualization is a tremendous technique for creating a positive approach to the future of your career. Many people think they cannot visualize sufficiently well to make a difference but this is rarely true.

Insight

To test yourself, try this:

Close your eyes and imagine the front door of your home. What colour is it? What colour is the door surround? Do you have a post box or knocker? Describe it. If you are able to visualize and describe your front door then you have the ability to use visualization to its full effect.

The value of visualization is that, as you visualize your future and see yourself in your new role, whether that is in a new career, new surroundings or in your current situation but loving the job, you will subconsciously start to make this happen. The mind is very powerful and does not know the difference between reality and fiction. Consequently if you tell it something is so, then it is. Create a visualization of the person you want to be and you will start to become that person. However, it is important that the visualization is a strong and powerful one. Read through Activity 20 in Part four of this book to take full advantage of this stunning technique.

Visualizations should be:

▶ regular – Try to visualize the same situation two or three times a day
▶ vivid – Exaggerate the colours and textures, try to notice any smells and feelings
▶ ambitious – See yourself acting and being the person you want to be or performing in the way you want to
▶ practised while relaxed – Only repeat when you are in a relaxed state. Your mind will be more receptive and you will be able to enjoy the visualization more.

GETTING YOUR BREATHING RIGHT

Now that we have the mind in focus we can start to think about how our energy manifests itself and how we can get more of the controlled energy we need to succeed.

Breathing is something that we take for granted but breathing effectively is a skill. Ask any singer or musician of wind instruments and they will tell you that they had to learn to breathe all over again for complete mastery of either their voice or instrument.

You also need this mastery as you will be heard regularly as you make yourself more visible, and in addition, your breathing controls how much energy you have.

Let's look at this in more detail. In a panic attack your breathing becomes very shallow and oxygen is not moving effectively around the lungs and heart. This will result in you having difficulty in speaking and moving. Keep your breathing deep, strong and steady and you will maintain your energy levels.

Good breathing techniques can also help with inner strength.

Try this exercise:

1 Stand with your feet shoulder width apart, arms loosely by your side.
2 Take a deep breath in through the nose to the count of three.
3 Hold the breath also for a count of three.
4 Now slowly breathe out through the mouth also to the count of three.

After performing this exercise a couple of times, try to slow the out-breath to the count of four – this way you will gain real control.

As you do this, feel your shoulders relax and your body becoming firm on the ground.

When you have completed this several times you will notice that you suddenly feel so much more relaxed, in control and 'grounded'. In fact you are and if proof were needed, ask a colleague to try and push you following this exercise. You will find that you are almost rooted into the ground, like a tree.

This exercise is wonderful for gaining additional personal power, perhaps in preparation for a negotiation. Also it will make you feel strong, confident and infallible just before a presentation or an interview.

BODY POSTURE

As we are slowly moving down the body we now need to consider our body posture. Body posture has been mentioned throughout this book because it is so important both in how we feel and how we represent ourselves to others. Doing the breathing exercise in the previous section has less impact if we then proceed to walk around the workplace looking like we shouldn't be there. Your body needs to be a representation of your confidence and suitability for the career you have chosen.

Many of us are not very aware of how we move and interact. Very few workplaces have mirrors, and if they did we might be quite surprised at what we see of ourselves. However, becoming body aware is the first step to considering how our bodies can actually help us.

Firstly, better posture can help us to breathe more effectively (and we have seen how that can help you in the previous section). Secondly, a good posture will enable good digestion. This means that you will get all the nutrients into your body effectively, thereby feeding your body and preparing it for action. Thirdly, good posture will give you confidence – even if you are nervous. It is a strange phenomenon that you instantly feel better (and stronger) when you stand tall.

Insight

Great posture will instantly knock pounds off your figure and you will immediately look younger. Try sitting, standing and moving with good posture for a week and see the results.

Finally, a top tip here is to watch other people in more senior positions. In other words do a little people watching. How do they move, walk and represent themselves with their body? Would that style work for you? Should you be modelling your postural movements on someone else?

FITNESS AND EATING WELL

It would be impossible to mention the body without considering fitness and food intake. Food and exercise are the maintenance system for our bodies. Just getting yourself in shape and thinking about how the food you eat affects you can give you great body awareness, and instantly you become more attentive to what you are doing and how you are eating.

As I said before, it is so easy to fill up on ready meals and junk food, but do these meals contain the goodness and nutrients required for carrying you through a long period of change, or the challenge of undertaking a qualification?

Eating well makes us feel fit and ready to roll. It also sends implicit messages to our brain that we value ourselves, and this also reinforces our confidence. Don't be found slumped over a computer at lunchtime with a sad and limp sandwich – it conveys so much about how you undervalue yourself.

RESILIENCE

The road to a new career or further up the development ladder is rarely smooth. You cannot expect everyone to be pleased for you and you may even find that some people are jealous of your new-found excitement and enthusiasm. It is not rare for others to heap

84

criticism on those who appear to be happy and succeeding. The green-eyed monster comes out to play and someone decides to put you back in your place. This is where being able to build resilience is vitally important. If you give in at the first slip then you will not progress very far. Life is full of banana skins and you have to learn ways of picking yourself up, dusting yourself down, and getting back on with the job in hand, otherwise you will not progress far.

This idea of building resilience can vary in different situations. For some people who become stressed quite easily this can mean looking at how they manage their own stress, while for others building resilience means being able to turn the other cheek and the ability to refrain from retaliating. Both of these are usually expressed through outward behaviour (anger, hurt) but in some individuals the lack of resilience is taken internally and manifests as a bodily condition such as colitis or irritable bowel syndrome. Neither is helpful as internal conditions will result in illness (see Activity 21 in Part four of this book) and external behaviour is usually unwelcome, leaving you to appear out of control. Certainly not good for someone who is trying to impress.

Trying to tell yourself that you will not come up against pressure is futile and unrealistic. Being able to deal with life's ups and downs is far more useful – and it is this ability that will impress others. Work on your resilience and you will also find the key to longevity in any career.

Business toolkit

In this chapter you will learn:
- *techniques for perfecting your presentation*
- *how to approach people*
- *how to contain your nerves*

We have already established that your future career move lies with other people, but those people need to be persuaded. To make a suggestion or approach any key member of staff, you will need to be sure of your pitch. Suddenly you are the product and you will need to present ideas as to how you (in this new role) can benefit the organization. You must do this in the right way. If you think through your delivery and plan in advance you increase your potential for acceptance by an additional 50 per cent. Rush in with no forethought and you are very likely to mumble, fumble and fail to get your message across.

How to approach people with ideas

WHAT IDEAS ARE WE TALKING ABOUT?

You want to improve your career and that could be with the company you already work for or with another company. Do not restrict your search to jobs that are advertised. It could be that you have seen an opportunity or can envisage a new role as being essential in six months' time. Maybe your dream job is already there but perhaps it does not (as yet) exist. Again perhaps you can see some potential for another post or role that is just not being filled by the current incumbent – or maybe someone's role is just too large for them to cope.

People sometimes miss the most obvious situations that are sitting right under their nose. They fail to see that an employee is struggling with too great a workload, and that the job needs dividing (producing a new post), that a new role needs to be created to deal with a specific new problem (another new post), or that an additional person focused solely on one aspect of the business can bring in greater rewards (another new and different post). For these reasons we need to find a way of tactfully raising the suggestion of these posts, but in a way that maintains the self-esteem of others, and pushes forward our own suggestions. It is critical that in approaching someone with an idea, you are happy to let them come to the conclusion that they had been thinking this all along.

WIIFM

No one wants to be told that they don't understand their business, especially if they are the owner and have built up and nurtured it from creation. It is therefore important that any approach we make is handled with tact and diplomacy.

Firstly, you need to ensure your facts are correct. You cannot say, 'If you make me your sales manager I will double your sales overnight' if you cannot quantify that. This is not a game show and you are trying to build an ethical career, not win a prize in bravado. Very occasionally you will hear of someone who stuck their neck out, made a bold promise and carried it off – but it is rare to be successful. It's far easier to make your approach in a sensible, factual manner and with evidence.

Secondly, make sure your facts are in order by finding out as much as you can about the situation before diving in. Ask other employees who have been there longer about the history of that post, whether they ever thought of trying this or that, and what was the outcome. This will prepare you for the 'We've tried that before. What makes you think this will be different?' response. If this has been tried before there must have been a reason why it was not successful – concentrate on that and think about a more workable solution. What could you bring that would make the situation this time completely different? Perhaps you have a proven record in a similar situation in your past employment, or a network of customers you have not revealed.

Thirdly, consider 'what's in it for me' (WIIFM). In other words, why would they want to do this? Any change in the business takes effort and if you are asking the owners of a business (or your manager) to create a job just for you, they need to know that there is something in it for them – a payback. No one is going to create your dream job just because you want it – but they might if they can see it will either benefit the business or themselves.

Lastly, reduce their personal risk: 'If you are not happy that this is working we can always go back to the way things are' or 'How about trying this for three months?' This means there is very little risk in them trying out the idea, and if they don't think it is working they can go back to square one.

Use the four points in this section to sketch out possible approaches to your ideas so that you are prepared for any reaction.

THE 'ELEVATOR' SPEECH

Some people just won't give you the time to even air your ideas. You may be dying to point out how creating one post would change the way that the unit is driven, or to suggest putting yourself forward for a project, but they keep saying, 'Come back to me later.' What do you do? When you come back later it appears that they have forgotten the entire idea. In these situations you need the elevator speech. This is so called because you need to convey your pitch in the time it takes an elevator to get to someone's desired floor. This approach is recommended to consultants when they want to convey some information to a possible client but find themselves constantly rebuffed. The notion is to corner the person in the elevator at which point you have roughly between 30 seconds and two minutes to present a short pitch. This needs to be practised and honed as you need to convey the important facts in the shortest amount of time possible. (For a full insight into the elevator speech, see Activity 22 in Part four of this book.)

You may not want to restrict yourself to elevators but the theory is a good one, as you may be in a situation where you need to sell yourself quickly and with impact. The other aspect of this technique is the element of surprise which can work in your favour. Being direct can sometimes reap rewards. After being impressed by a speaker at an event, I waited until he had finished, approached him and directly told him that I wanted to work for him. My colleagues were confounded by my approach – he was certainly surprised – but three months later I was offered a job. Sometimes a bold gesture pays off.

THE DRIP, DRIP METHOD

If you are already working in the organization then persistence can really pay off. The drip, drip method is simply this: the constant dripping (or repetition) of information from many different sources all point to the same outcome. What you are aiming for here is that the manager hears the same (or a very similar) message from several different sources. It can work very well with resistant people. The first time they hear it they may be dismissive, but rather than give up, you make sure they hear the same message again from other people and in other arenas. Through gentle, but constant dripping they will find that it will become acceptable to them after all – if so many people say it must be so, then it is probably right!

THE BUILDING BLOCK METHOD

This is where you build up to the solution in much slower steps and your ultimate aim is to enable the manager or business owner to think that it was their idea all along. It is similar to the drip, drip method but instead of repetition the steps build on each other, starting very low and not mentioning a solution for a while. Therefore the first few comments may just be hinting at the problem in an 'I wonder if ...' kind of way, as if you are musing in your own mind. The solution may not come for some time yet.

THE BOARDROOM DAZZLER

We must not forget that some larger ideas may require a full presentation in the boardroom to convey their complexity and introduce new roles. Presenting does not come naturally to everyone and that is why it is covered in more detail in the following section. However, the approach bears a mention here because in some situations only the boardroom is appropriate. For example, if you were presenting on how to run a new part of the business or how a project would operate (including mentioning some key roles that would need to be created) your management team/decision-makers/ shareholders would expect a more formal communication at one of their monthly board meetings. Within the presentation you have a considerable opportunity to be influential, but again pre-thought and planning are essential.

Whether you decide on a subtle method of influence or a more direct approach will very much depend on your situation and whom you want to influence. One of the greatest keys to influencing others is personal credibility, and therefore always endeavour to be sincere and professional. It does not matter what your current job is, if you have an idea you want to convey don't hold back. Think about the most appropriate method for getting your ideas across, and go for it.

Presentation perfect

Most jobs today will require you to perform some activity to demonstrate your skill in action. One of the most popular is the presentation. This is for a number of reasons including the following:

- ▶ Many jobs now require this skill as part of their daily activity
- ▶ Your presentation will demonstrate how persuasive you are
- ▶ How you structure your presentation will demonstrate how logically you can structure your point of view, and also your organizational skills
- ▶ Presentations demonstrate confidence.

Unfortunately presentations are one of the most feared aspects of many people's jobs and can have you running for the hills. However, let's turn this to our advantage ...

Rather than run away from presentations, if we can learn to work with them we can take advantage of a few of the benefits they bring. For a start, if so many people avoid them then that is all for the good, there will be fewer people going for the job. (Fact: introduce any form of testing and some applicants will drop out of the selection process.) Further, if we can pull off a credible presentation that we can be sure will be enjoyed by those present then we are more than halfway to securing the job. (Fact: People who can deliver great presentations are always popular with employers.) Let's get started ...

However, a word of caution first. Creating an effective presentation for an interview is fairly easy but you need to find out whether presentations will be a regular part of the job and in what circumstances (In-work, for the board? Outside to customers?

Large-scale presentations in theatres or to small groups?).
Performing a one-off presentation for an interview is very different from presenting regularly. You would not want to find yourself in a position of being constantly stressed out by one aspect of your job that does not suit your personality.

WHAT MAKES A GOOD PRESENTATION?

When you are asked to provide a presentation during interview, the panel are looking for:

▶ the choice of topic if there is one – which you chose and why
▶ how the presentation is structured
▶ any interesting points you make or how you argue your case
▶ how you interact with the equipment
▶ your fluency of speech (including how you convey complex information)
▶ how you present yourself (and would therefore represent the company).

This may appear a scary list but the secret here is to cut through all that by keeping things simple. The more complexity you introduce, the more there is to go wrong.

THE TOPIC

Let's start with the topic. You may be given a topic or you might have to choose one. (If you are asked to choose, at some point you will be asked to justify your selection so be sure of why you chose the topic you did.) The topic is likely to be either a product (their key product or the company itself) or a concept/personal view (present your view of education today). On the rare occasion you are asked to choose your own topic, select something you know about but which can also tell the audience a little-known fact or some further information. This is not the time to try and research something completely new as that would create further tension on the day and you may well find that you have an expert in the audience.

Using a hobby or pastime is fine as long as you:

▶ create an interesting angle on it (instead of 'My Hobby – Sailing' focus on 'Six of the most useful sailing knots, and how they can be used')

▶ have some interesting facts to introduce ('This knot, although deceptively simple, was the one used at the Battle of Trafalgar to secure the …').

STRUCTURING YOUR PRESENTATION

Remember the 'keep it simple' motto. Firstly, how long should your presentation be? You should be provided with a timescale, and if they are interviewing approximately six people that day, it will probably be no longer than 15 minutes. With set-up and feedback time, six presentations are going to take at least three hours to view (and that is with everyone timed to perfection). That is a lot to sit through!

Given that you have indeed been given 15 minutes, you will need to introduce yourself and the topic, and at the end bring the talk to a neat close. Both of those sections should take around two to three minutes each, leaving you around ten minutes for the main body of your talk. Ask yourself these questions:

▶ What is the main aspect/point I need to convey?
▶ If I need to explain a complex idea, how can I break the information down into manageable chunks?
▶ What metaphors can I use to convey stories, ideas and thoughts?

If you are using media presentation slides you will need approximately two to three minutes of speaking per slide. Therefore, for a ten-minute body you will need only four or five slides (after the introductory slide and final slide) to display while you speak. Put only bullet points on the slides so that they are an aide-mémoire and you are not tempted to read them out verbatim. If you know your subject well, you only need prompts to keep you on track.

Your presentation should now be like a story: an introduction, a journey taking the audience through a progressive story or argument, through to a conclusion or closure.

Finally, try to run to time. Some recruiters are a stickler for this as speaking to time is a skill in itself and to overrun is very rude to the next speaker.

MEDIA INTERACTION

If you are not sure how to use media presentation tools, find out. Most organizations will let you have a few minutes to attune yourself to their equipment. However, keep gimmicks to a minimum. I was recently asked to present with slides that contained a considerable amount of animation. Unfortunately, when I went to the venue the equipment they had did not support the animation and I was left with motionless slides that suddenly appeared a little odd.

Do you like to stand still or move around when you talk? The amount to which you are able to move around could easily depend on whether you have to stand behind a lectern or wear a microphone. Remember – the presentation is supposed to convey your personality, and therefore some movement and gestures are good. Be yourself as that is how you will feel most comfortable.

PERSONAL PRESENTATION

Your accent is immaterial but clarity is vital, as is how you convey your ideas. Basically you are communicating and if the audience does not understand your points, you will have failed. For this reason we are back to 'keeping it simple' once again. An interview is not the time to take risks.

You do not have to wear a suit but be smart and comfortable (this is not the moment to break in a new pair of shoes or wear some item that is clearly too tight or uncomfortable). If you are aware of your nervousness creating a rash on your chest or around the neck area (this is very common), do not wear low or open necks because this will only make the situation worse, as you become aware of the rash (and therefore your nervousness) being visible to everyone.

COMBATING NERVES

A certain amount of adrenalin will sharpen your presentation and keep you edgy. It is therefore quite good to feel excited and keen just before a presentation, but when this cascades into fear, nerves can paralyze your performance.

Some useful tips for managing your nerves are:

▶ Prepare and practise as much as possible before the event. Many of the situations you may fear can be eradicated through careful preparation.

- ▶ Think about what you are going to wear. Be comfortable and if you think you might perspire heavily, keep a jacket on.
- ▶ Hum on the journey there to warm up your voice.
- ▶ Run your wrists under cold water just before going on as the skin is thinnest there and will cool the blood around your body.
- ▶ Apply roll-on antiperspirant to your palms if you find that your hands sweat with nerves.
- ▶ Try a little mental trick: tell yourself that you are just the warm-up act, that the next speaker is the main one, so there is no need to be so scared as they will pay you far less attention.
- ▶ Try some self-psychology and put this in perspective: ask yourself on a scale of 1 to 10 where does this presentation lie on the scale of the worst thing that can happen? (1 is 'OK', and 10 is total, all-out panic!)
- ▶ For two or three minutes before you speak, look skywards with your eyes and think through your worst fears. It is almost impossible to feel frightened when you are looking upwards.

9

···

New ideas outside work

In this chapter you will learn:
- **the benefits of looking outside your own company**
- **how to approach other companies**
- **how to inspire others**

In this part of the book you are planning your career future, a future that may be within or outside your current place of work. We have to be realistic here: even if there is the type of job you want inside your current organization, lack of staff movement or cutbacks in expansion may mean that your chances of even trying for the job of your dreams are just not likely to come about. You may be looking on with envy but find that you are miles away from this being an actuality. If this is your situation then you will have to start researching other organizations.

Researching other organizations

LOCATING OPPORTUNITIES

Start with the 'type' of business or industry where you might find your job. If you are looking for a more senior position in administration it is very likely that many large organizations will have these positions, but if you are looking for something very specific (for example, a position as a film editor) you will have to target your search towards that specific industry.

Not all geographical locations house equal numbers of the same opportunities. For example, the need for teachers is widely spread but IT companies are more prevalent in certain areas of the country. Some organizations also need to be located 'where it's at' and therefore it is no surprise that many PR companies have offices in London. This might mean that if you want a job in a specific industry you may have to think about relocating. If you feel this might be you, think about this carefully, especially if it means leaving family and friends. It could be the opportunity of a lifetime but you may also feel isolated. It has to be your decision.

To find out who and what companies are available in your area or county, visit your local library, Job Centre and/or Chamber of Commerce. They will all be able to tell you where organizations are based that might have your desired type of job.

RESEARCH

When you have located a selection of companies that you are interested in, you need to do some further research. The internet is very helpful with research and most organizations now have their own internet site that includes a business plan that you can usually download to find out how the business is progressing. If you read the business plan you will be able to find out the direction of share prices and profitability, and whether there are any plans for expansion. In a multinational organization you may find that some areas are expanding while others are diminishing. Look for areas of development and see if there are opportunities there. Look also at the organizational values and ensure they match your own. It can be very uncomfortable to find yourself in a business that does not match your value structure (see Activity 23 in Part four of this book). If a business plan is not available on their website, contact the organization and ask for a business plan to be sent to you. Try to look at a few organizations so that you can compare opportunities. You are investing a considerable amount of time and interest in your career and you want to make the right decisions – and you can only do that with sufficient information.

MAKING CONTACT

It is now up to you to make direct contact. There are a number of ways you can do this:

▶ Write to the HR department – This is very safe and easy but you might find that they 'file your interest' and do nothing else. HR staff will know about which jobs are being offered at the current time, but they do not have the full picture about what could be needed in the future, and they are not particularly interested in creating jobs to capture talent for the future.

▶ Write to the departmental manager – You may find this is a slightly better approach if you are hoping to capture their attention. Being cheeky can often intrigue but if you are going to take this approach, make sure you don't over-sell yourself (tell the truth) and ensure you have thought through your next move. (Departmental managers and directors work very quickly. They may offer you a job there and then and would expect you to take it.)

▶ Ask someone from your desired department to have a meeting (or a coffee) with you – This approach works quite well because it is non-threatening on both sides. You can find out more about the business and how opportunities arise and they can chat in the full knowledge that nothing is promised. Ring in the first instance and introduce yourself, and then explain what you would like. If you feel more comfortable, you can put this in an email. Initially ask for just 15 or 30 minutes of their time, and be clear what you want to talk about. If they refuse, ask if there is anyone else you could contact.

▶ Professional meetings – These are often run by professional bodies such as a Chartered Institute. You don't have to be a member to attend and you can go as a guest for the evening. Some organizations also host the evenings, and when they do they encourage their own staff to attend too. It might be that you are able to make a contact or two during the evening, so carry your business cards just in case.

▶ Trade exhibitions – Most counties have regular (local) business exhibitions (if you are unsure ask your local Chamber of Commerce) where you can visit various stands. The entry is usually free and it is a chance for businesses to find out about and to make contact with each other. As many companies take a stand to have a presence there, you may find your desired organization is represented. If so you can start networking by chatting to the people on the stand itself. They are always eager to explain their business to you.

▶ Mentoring – Approach a manager from your desired organization to see whether they would be willing to provide some mentoring for you. These could be one- or two-hour slots where you meet to discuss problems you have in your career and request help in finding the right avenue for you. The benefits of mentoring are that you will be able to find out all about the other organization, other people's experience, and the ins and outs of the various jobs and career opportunities without having to leave your current role. Should a vacancy then arise in your desired organization you are in the right place and possibly have some contacts already.

INTERNET SEARCHES

The internet has completely changed the way that we interact with other people and businesses. It can help you to locate names and addresses so that you can focus on contacting the right people immediately. However, do be very wary of who you interact with on the internet and be cautious about giving out too much personal data. Although a very useful research tool, the internet is also very good at hiding someone's real identity and you need to be careful when posting personal data. Using the internet you can conduct and contact the following:

▶ Job searches – Either look for job opportunities or post your CV online (but check with the organization as to how companies access information and whether it is open to abuse)
▶ Agencies – Most job agencies are now online and you can sign up without having to visit them
▶ HQ – If you are thinking of a move to a large organization look on their headquarters' site. Their job opportunities are often posted up there first.
▶ Social networking – Check out if the company you want to work for has a social networking site. If it is a large organization it will have a strong internet presence, so search on their name.

Boosting your skills portfolio

At times of change it can be very easy to take your foot off the accelerator of learning – after all, you don't really know what you will need in your new position, do you? No good starting something in case it is the wrong programme. Perhaps you should get the job first and then concentrate on collecting a new skills set. If you are tempted to think like this STOP! It would be a huge mistake for three reasons:

▶ You are allowing time to drip by without learning anything – literally wasting time *and* during this lull you are losing the habit of learning
▶ So many skills are transferable that all new skills are useful, even if they do not initially appear directly relevant to your new career
▶ Employers these days look for staff who take responsibility for their own self-development, and don't leave it to others.

Times of change are exactly the right time to be thinking of increasing your skills portfolio and developing yourself for the next part of your career journey. The very nature of learning and thinking through how you will apply those skills will concentrate your thoughts on your job and therefore provide you with a sharp focus. For example, if you are learning about negotiating techniques you may think that you do not have much need for that currently in your job, but it is always useful to learn how to negotiate a higher salary or the best price for a car, and while you are contemplating this you are concentrating on your job once again.

GENERIC SKILLS

Generic skills are skills that cover a multitude of organizations and situations. They include such skills as:

▶ negotiating
▶ customer care
▶ dealing with difficult people
▶ numeracy
▶ communication
▶ report and letter writing
▶ time management ...

... and so forth. These skills are going to be useful in any situation and used within most jobs – therefore if you are up-skilling in any of these areas, your CV will be enhanced for any employer, now or in the future.

TRANSFERABLE SKILLS

Transferable skills are skills that can be transferred from one situation to another. For example, you may find that in one job you are trained to run a budget for the admin team. Those numeracy skills are very useful when you decide to make a move into the finance department of another organization. The only problem you can see is that they are looking for staff with a background in finance, and you feel your limited experience only scratches the surface. You may feel that you cannot claim financial knowledge – or you may not apply at all, which would be real shame because you could claim your budgeting experience as a transferable skill. When completing the application form, and at the interview, you could mention your budget experience in a way that shows it is not exactly the depth of experience they would like, but that it has the same roots and underlying skills. Clearly if you are able to run budgets, and enjoy the process, you have a head for finance and that might just get you short-listed.

Transferable skills are useful for that reason: they allow us to move into similar roles and specialisms by sharing the underlying skills base, and claim experience in areas where we might not have a complete fit in terms of skills, knowledge and/or experience.

A BIT ABOUT IT SKILLS

If you have been guilty of sticking your head in the sand on this one, make no mistake – IT is here to stay! It has developed fast and is not going away. If you are not sure of your IT skills or you missed out on this vital piece of personal learning, there are plenty of government-backed programmes to get you up to date and running. Any employer would expect you to come into their organization knowing how to use a computer, if only to search for information. You don't need qualifications for general use but make sure your skills and abilities are current and that you can use popular software and access the internet. There are many free and subsidized schemes available to you if you feel out of date, and there are computers in libraries for general use if you don't currently own one.

POLISHING OFF YOUR CV

I have mentioned your CV several times but I make no apologies for mentioning it again here. Be honest, do you have it to hand? Hunt it out now – can you locate it in 30 seconds?

Your CV should not just be a document that you dig out and update when you want to look for another job – it is too important to be languishing on some unused computer drive somewhere or worse, a limp paper copy, hidden in a drawer. In the first instance your CV makes a great repository for listing skills. Where else can you store a list of your qualifications, skills and experience that is accessible and easy to carry everywhere – just in case you need it urgently? Yes, you might have built up a portfolio of certificates or evidence but it is hardly transportable and I am sure you do not carry it around with you.

Maintaining an up-to-date CV is also helpful for another reason. How many times have you been faced with a blank application form and felt overwhelmed? What month did I start that job? What year were those qualifications? Dates are so difficult to remember and if you are completing every application form from scratch you are making the task so much more difficult than it needs to be. Completing any number of forms is ten times easier if you have all the information in front of you.

If you are at all unsure about creating the right CV or feel that perhaps your CV is out of date, look at Activity 24 in Part four of this book. There you will find out how to create the right CV for your needs and to attract future prospects.

Extending your skills outside the workplace

There may be occasions where you find it more difficult to secure opportunities to extend your skills inside the workplace. Not all organizations have training departments or support training staff in anything other than the statutory essentials, such as health and safety training. There is also the argument touted by some organizations that question why they would want to train their staff in top skills if they then go on to secure better jobs elsewhere. In other organizations you may not be able to undertake training in any area that you don't have experience in. This makes it very difficult for you to gain a job in management with a low level of experience because according to this ruling you cannot access the training until you are in a management post!

If you are in any of these situations you will have to look for opportunities to build your experience and skills outside the organization. Fortunately this is not as difficult as it might at first appear.

VOLUNTEERING

Many organizations welcome volunteers who will undertake a whole range of tasks. Volunteering is not just about standing near shops, shaking tins and organizing collections. There are opportunities for teamwork and management practice, in addition to the many practical skills that are always needed.

COMMUNITY CLUBS

There are many clubs that can help grow and practise skills. For example, the Rotary Club, Women's Institute, Round Table, Soroptimists and your local hospital League of Friends are all countrywide, guaranteeing you a branch near to where you live. Many of these organizations also offer the opportunity to network with other professional business people and will help you gain not only a new set of friends but also a new set of contacts. They may have regular talks with speakers too, offering you the opportunity to learn from others in addition to, perhaps, speaking yourself.

POLITICS AND ACTION GROUPS

There are many political and/or action groups around the country and therefore if you feel passionately about a particular issue, you may find a forum where you can increase your skills in a range of ways including debating, speaking, marketing and newspaper and magazine work.

Just one word of warning. Check on the level of militancy of any group you join. You would not want your new membership to work against you in the job stakes.

HOLDING A COMMUNITY POST

Within the community there are many positions held by people just like you. The positions are often unpaid (apart from expenses) but offer great scope for development and many offer the very training that you may be unable to access at work. If you have ever thought of becoming a magistrate, rural warden, Community Police Officer or joining the Royal National Lifeboat Institute then you will also have the satisfaction of knowing that your work benefits the community in addition to growing your skills portfolio.

Change your tabloid newspaper for a broadsheet. Pick up a journal instead of a magazine. Open the dictionary and learn a new word every day – and then practise it in context. Visit the library and select a classic text or a book on philosophy. In other words, step out of your regular reading pattern and into a different (and more challenging) world.

So often we exist in our own cosy world that does not stretch us and feels very safe. However, although this feels comfortable if we are not careful we start to become used to this cosseted existence. It is rather like treading water when you need to be stretching out for a swim if you are ever to reach the far side of the shore. Not all skills are activity based. There is great skill in having a nimble mind and being able to analyse facts, of knowing recent political and world history smattered with a general appreciation of philosophy. Employers need to know that you have a view on the world, and that you are a driver in life, not just a passenger.

Using a career coach

If you were going on a journey to somewhere unknown, where you did not know the people, the language or even the quickest way to get there, meeting someone with prior knowledge and a network of contacts would be very helpful. You would be able to shortcut problems, find faster routes, speak the right language and find your way through to your chosen destination so much more quickly and more easily. You would have someone to ask questions of when you became lost, and someone to share your frustrations with – you might even discover more about yourself and have fun on the way! That is a similar experience to using a career coach.

Career coaches have trodden the path before you. They know the shortcuts and how best to present yourself for maximum impact. They can, in one hour, hone your CV, give you a route to follow (and possibly even some contacts), and provide support and expert knowledge that will leave you with an action plan to follow. In essence, a condensed boost of energy targeted directly at your career. However, always ask for an estimation of cost before entering into a long-term commitment.

TAKING THE CHALLENGE

Using a career coach is not an easy ride. Coaches are there to challenge you and make you really think about what you want, why you want it and how you think this career will solve all your problems or answer your dreams. Although they may cut through many processes or share ideas that you may not have thought of, they will not do the thinking for you. Your coach will treat your sessions as learning opportunities and an opportunity for reflection and development. Be in no doubt that you will feel challenged and stretched in your thinking, but that what emerges will be a clearer sense of who you are, where you are going and how you are going to get there.

FINDING THE RIGHT CAREER COACH

Like anything in life that involves people, there can be some variety in quality. Some coaches are self-taught and others are trained, some are focused on you 'finding yourself' while others are focused on getting you a job – any job. This is why you should speak to several coaches before settling to work with one.

To find a number of possible coaches:

► look in local papers
► ask friends and colleagues
► ask at work
► contact your local Job Centre
► enquire through large agencies
► enquire through outplacement consultancies
► contact a professional coaching or HR institute.

Most coaches will speak with you (even if only by phone) before you book any sessions because they know how important it is to find the right match. You need to know that your coach has the right background, skills and techniques, career knowledge and contacts to make this a valuable experience for you. Paying for the services of a career coach is one thing but you are investing far more of your time, energy and dreams so do not rush this part of the process. Similarly if they believe that you are not sufficiently committed or that they cannot help you, they may also withdraw. The match must be right for both of you for it to be effective.

THE CONTRACT

Most coaches will request that a contract is drawn up between you, detailing the commitments you are both making. This is a very important part of the process because as you go through coaching the focus can change. For example, you may start out wanting a specific job but halfway through have a 'Eureka' moment and decide that you really want to be something completely different. The contract will allow for change but ensure that you are committed to progress.

Coaching is not an easy process. The process asks you to be committed to change, and it is easy to fall by the wayside when you have so much else going on in your life. Your coach will want to know how you are going to deal with situations like this and who else can support you – and all this will be included in the contract.

OUTCOMES

It can be helpful to draw up some outcomes you would like to achieve with your coach. For example, one of the areas that people often want to work on is their interview skills. It can be a long time between job changes and it is not uncommon to feel a little rusty in this area. This, coupled by the fact that you only get one chance at an interview, can result in it being fraught with tension. If this is you, then an outcome might be to 'ensure that I can perform persuasively in an interview'. This way your coach will be clear as to what is needed for the sessions to be a success.

THE TIMESCALE

Your coach should be able to predict how many sessions and over what time period you will need their assistance. Typically coaching is not an ongoing situation. It may be that you need three one-hour sessions, held fortnightly, or six two-hour sessions held monthly. Your coach should know what they aim to achieve at each of these sessions and how the coaching should flow. They should be able to give you a clear indication of the sessions at the first meeting, and this way you will be able to make a decision regarding the overall commitment.

Using psychometrics

Personality profiling can open up a whole new world in terms of you understanding your own personality and finding a career choice that is right for you. Working in a job that isn't a good fit for your personality type becomes stressful as you are working against your natural strengths. For example, someone who is naturally quiet and introverted might find it difficult to work in a sales environment. This does not mean that they cannot do it – just that it will cause them greater stress than someone who is more gregarious. This is why many recruitment organizations use psychometrics: they give an insight into the personality of the person in front of them and indicate possible suitability for many careers.

WHY WOULD I WANT TO USE PSYCHOMETRICS MYSELF?

The first reason was hinted at in the introduction to this section: if recruitment professionals use psychometrics then you need to be aware of what they are and how to feel comfortable completing them. It is very possible that you might be asked to complete a psychometric assessment as part of assessing your suitability for a post, and you will feel so much more relaxed and able to portray the real you if you have tried a few out beforehand.

The second reason is that psychometrics offer an insight into ourselves. Feedback from a psychometric instrument is often used in coaching as part of the road towards understanding your true self and how that manifests as behaviour. With psychometrics you are the person ticking the boxes or making the selection – it is your view of you – not someone else's view of you. Because of this you need good-quality feedback to place your view of yourself in context, such as why you might see certain aspects of your personality as strong or weak, and how that might be interpreted by others.

Some psychometrics are also developmentally based. This means that they are not there to categorize you but specifically targeted to help you develop certain areas or skills, and these can be filed with your CV to demonstrate that you take your own development seriously and if undertaken annually they can show personal progression over a period of time.

WHAT ARE THEY GOING TO MEASURE?

Many people fear psychometrics because they believe that they will reveal something about their personality that they would rather not let others know. Let me lay to rest the idea that you can be categorized as a bad person, selfish or untidy just from psychometrics. Psychometric instruments are totally non-judgemental and so are not looking for this type of measure. Most psychometric instruments are based around The Big Five. These are five measures that assess levels of:

▶ extroversion – This means the amount to which you like to gain energy from the outside world, integrating with others and sharing ideas

▶ neuroticism/anxiety – This aims to measure how excited or anxious you become around work tasks

▶ openness to experience/conformity – This aims to measure whether you are a 'corporate beast' or more 'maverick'

▶ agreeableness/tenderness versus tough mindedness – Aims to measure the extent to which you follow others and are able to take decisions independently

▶ conscientiousness – This is the amount to which you are able to focus on your work and pay attention to detail.

As you can imagine, all of these measures could be interpreted in a positive or negative fashion, depending on context. In addition to the measures in this list, different psychometric questionnaires are targeted differently. For example, some are more general and provide an insight to your personality, others may be targeted more towards those who want a specific career choice, such as indicating whether you are suited to a career in customer care.

FEEDBACK REALIZATION

After receiving feedback take time out to consider the implications. Feedback is so individual that you may want to ask more questions or just think about the data for a while. You may find that you are not as suited to the job as you thought, or that maybe you should be focusing your energies in a different direction. Only you can relate the outcome of a psychometric measure to your situation, and that can take some time. I advise all people receiving feedback to put the report in a drawer for a week and then read it again, highlighting any areas you are unsure about and need clarification.

For many people, psychometrics can answer so many questions such as why certain jobs are not for them or why they feel uncomfortable in their current job, in addition to where they would be most suited.

WHERE DOES THE INFORMATION GO?

You should be offered personal feedback. It is not good practice to either be given the report on its own or for your report to be sent to the company without you knowing the contents. Your feedback should be by a specialist who is registered with that particular psychometic tool provider to give feedback. This ensures you receive feedback from someone who understands how the psychometric tool has been constructed, and how each of the measures can be interpreted. In addition the person giving you the feedback should tell you exactly what will happen to your report. Usually you will be given a copy of your report to keep, and the interviewing organization will also have a copy to refer to for this process. Check that the copy they keep is destroyed after the interview as Data Protection should preclude them maintaining a copy for a long period of time without informing you of this.

If you are either commissioning your own psychometric tests or if you are trying a few out (in other words there is no employer involved) you will still need feedback, and at the end of that meeting your report should be handed back to you.

IDENTIFYING OPPORTUNITIES

So now your antennae are up and you are on the lookout. You have done the activities, narrowed your field of vision and selected an area you would like to work in. I say 'area' and not specific job because there may be a whole host of similar supporting jobs that surround main ones. For example in the film and television industry there are probably jobs you have never even heard of until you start to look in depth. I once met a man at a party whose job was to design construction models for a plastic brick company. He admitted he was the envy of all 'boys who never grew up' the world over. When I asked him how he found this job (because I had never heard of it or seen anything like this advertised) he told me that he joined the company in another job, and then moved across when he discovered the job of his dreams was actually real. His message was that jobs like this are just not advertised. Therefore, don't discard other opportunities in the same industry or business area – they could lead to you being offered the job you always wanted.

Taking time to smell the roses

Deciding to take your career in hand can result in you being highly focused and centred on attaining your goal to the exclusion of all other things. Some of you will be very successful but others may not be, and that could be for a host of reasons (such as there being little movement in the industry, or the job you want being so poorly paid that you cannot take it at this moment). It would be easy to begin to feel bitter or resent all the efforts you have made for what seems like little or no reward. Unfortunately, life does not come with any guarantees but one way we can put ourselves in the right mindset for positive recovery is to visualize our career as a journey rather than a destination.

Life moves fast enough without us concentrating only on the outcomes we desire. There is so much in life to live, love and learn on your travels. Focus too tightly on the destination and you are likely to miss the glorious scenery to be had along the way. Instead take time to 'smell the roses' and you might just find you adjust your thinking as you go – and you will enjoy the journey so much more.

MAKING FRIENDS AND CONTACTS

You can never have too many friends or contacts – it is simply impossible. Be sociable with everyone and gather friends as you go. Keep in touch by sending cards or building your own social network site. You never know where other people may move to, and whom they may meet later on. You are creating a social web of contacts that will continue to grow and will pay off in the future.

LEARNING NEW SKILLS

Take every opportunity to learn *anything* and *everything* (as long as it is not illegal or dangerous). You never know where a skill may take you. The more you know (knowledge) and can do (skills) the better conversationalist you will be. There is no such thing as a waste of time in terms of learning. (If you are sent on a course and you truly find the subject boring, then concentrate on the people and network like crazy.)

REFINING YOUR THINKING

Create miniature goals so that you can assess your progress along the way. See these as pit stops that allow you to ask yourself, 'How much progress have I made?', 'Is this still what I want?', 'What should the next step be?' and 'How can I make that happen?' If you have mini goals you can console yourself that you are moving nearer to your goal (even if everything appears to be taking forever).

LATERAL THINKING

There is always more than one way to get what you want in your career. If you find that you cannot enter into the business world of your choice, how about starting your own business? It might seem scary at first but most businesses start with one person and a dream or a passion. In other words if you cannot make it into a business, create that business. It might start as a hobby that pays but who knows where it could end up?

Inspiring others

This book has been about you. You are the centre of all the activities and the focus around which it has been written. Finding the right job for you can take a while and you might have to make a few sideways moves along the way, but like any journey you will learn a lot along the way. That knowledge must not be lost. Everyone who finds a career they enjoy should help and inspire others to do the same. If you progressed down the route of engaging a career coach you will know just how helpful another person can be – and now that you are that person you are in a position to help others.

When you inspire others to find the right career you can do so in the knowledge that you have given them a complete life skill – one that they can take with them for life. There is an old saying, 'Give someone a fish and they are fed for a day, teach someone to fish and they can feed themselves forever.' In passing on your journey, knowledge, skills and expertise, you are indeed teaching others to fish by providing tools and techniques they can take forward for the rest of their lives.

SHARING FEELINGS

Close your eyes for a moment and re-experience the feeling of being uncomfortable at work. Do you feel out of control? Lost and alone? Now switch that for the feeling of knowing where you want to get to in your career. Do you feel more certain, sure and confident?

When you can share and acknowledge those feelings in yourself you can start to share them with others that you wish to help. It is very powerful to empathize with someone and be able to say, 'I know how it feels to be in your position, not sure if this is the career for you. I felt …' This is how you link your communication with others at a deeper level of understanding. Acknowledge their feelings and show people a path forwards.

MENTORING AND COACHING

Throughout this book I have mentioned mentoring and coaching as something that might help you, but how would you feel about mentoring others? There can be a great deal of satisfaction in helping others through the same problems you have experienced and sharing their success. Most towns have mentoring schemes for young people too, and as work is such a large part of our lives, they would welcome some new input (many will even train you in mentoring if you feel unsure).

GOING A STAGE FURTHER

Many schools delight in having someone from business or industry come in to talk to the students and inspire them to reach for their dreams. Simply talking about how you became this or that is hugely interesting to those who have their full career ahead of them. Perhaps you can share some amusing stories and/or warn students of the 'potholes' you fell into along the way. Your inspiration can offer so much to others that it is a gift in itself – so don't hide yourself, get out there and share with the world. Life has a strange way of coming full circle.

PASS IT ON

If you have found this book helpful, pass it on. Knowledge is not meant to be kept to yourself; it is better shared. Give someone else the opportunity of changing their career goals and bathe in the satisfaction of helping them achieve that.

Case studies

CAROL

Carol decides that she has a number of ideas that Morgan Pilchard can implement to become more visible and help increase business. She reads up on the best way of presenting these ideas for maximum impact. She wants Mr Morgan to view her more professionally and see the contribution she can make. She undertakes a visualization exercise to ensure she gains more confidence and she checks her facts. Part of her presentation is that she is asking for greater responsibility but needs some support (possibly also some training) to make this a reality. Suddenly Carol seems energized into staying and being part of the key team that help build Morgan Pilchard into a market leader. She realizes that you don't have to leave to get a better job – sometimes it was there all the time.

SAMIA

Samia recognizes that she has to speak to someone about her plans and that she might have to give a presentation on her ideas. She has to sell herself if she wants to be considered for a job that, on the face of it, seems very different to her current one. However, she has thought about her transferable skills and she feels ready to put her case forward. Before doing so she reads a short book on project management to acquaint herself with the skills and terminology required. She also finds out that she can train for a recognized project management qualification as it is a career in itself, and she can join an institute. She is also feeling so confident that she feels that, even if the factory managers do not approve of her plan, she will pursue it anyway, either in her own time or with another organization because it feels so 'right' for her.

Samia feels that following on from her presentation she can then look at whether her marriage plans can go ahead, and feels sure that if there is a delay it will only be short term. However, if they do go forward she is sure that with project management as her focus her wedding will be the best managed wedding ever.

JASON

Jason has met with HR and they seem impressed with his attitude and suggestions. They tell him that they are going to be starting a supervisory training programme in a month's time but he will have to apply to his manager to be put forward.

Jason recognizes that he has not always been a model employee and so plans his case very carefully in line with the suggestions about approaching people. He knows he is young but he has also signed up for a weekly course on becoming a manager being run by his old school for senior pupils and parents.

Jason also wants to make sure that no one else from his old school can say that they were not warned to take more notice in class and so he decides that, when he becomes a supervisor the first thing he will do is volunteer to go back into his old school and talk to pupils. He feels young enough to still connect with them and thinks that they may listen to him. He would also like to work with the school on other enterprise projects that bring the factory and the school together – an interesting development from someone who did not want to stay in school a minute longer than necessary.

HENRI

Henri is suddenly very busy. He has to organize an interview presentation for a cruise liner agency and have some publicity photos taken. They also want his CV and so that needs to be polished and targeted towards promoting that side of his work.

Due to the recent surge in popularity in ballroom dancing, his local town has started regular tea dances. They asked for musicians and Henri put his name forward and is now booked to play once a week and is even paid for the privilege. He is also thinking of teaching the instrument in the future on a private lesson basis.

He has no stress symptoms and has decided that, although the large salary was nice, he would prefer from now on to work within his personal value system, helping others along the way. He still has enough income for essential life items and if he can secure a cruise liner talk once a year that can be his and Sarah's holiday. All round Henri is happier and more relaxed living the type of lifestyle many people would envy than ever before.

CHRIS

Chris visits the Job Centre and they offer to do a psychometric test to help her further. This type of test allows the user to see whether their demeanour is more suited to certain industries. The results of the test confirm what Chris was thinking, that a medical role would be very favourable and the careers adviser suggested that, given the rest of Chris's analysis that she shared, Chris should consider retraining as a maternity nurse. Chris is initially shocked – she had never thought of anything like this but the more she thinks about it, it does tick a lot of boxes and offer a great deal of job satisfaction. After all, even though there is never a guarantee of lifetime employment, women will continue to have babies and any nursing background is welcomed in many other professions. It will mean several years' study, but Chris can see the benefits. It is now for her to decide.

10 THINGS TO REMEMBER

1 Look after your body and find helpful ways of using mind techniques to give you more confidence and resilience.

2 Anyone can come up with great ideas – they are not the preserve of the elite. However, not everyone presents their ideas in the right way, at the right time, and they may be ignored because of this. Learn how to approach people with ideas and show everyone what you can contribute towards the organization.

3 Being able to give presentations gives you a head start because so many people are afraid of them. Simple techniques can ensure you present with style and at the same time demonstrate your great communication skills. If the word 'presentation' makes you jittery, change your mindset and think about it as a form of simple communication of your ideas. Instead of talking one-to-one, you will be talking one-to-several.

4 In your search for a future career cast your net wide. You may be lucky and find what you want on your doorstep, or you may need to go a little further. There are ways of testing out other organizations before you approach them – and you do not have to wait until they advertise their vacancies. It is amazing how jobs can be created for people where a senior manager or owner sees talent. Networks are never wasted.

5 Keep your skills up to date and relevant. While you are waiting for an opportunity, develop some new skill so that when the opportunity does arise, you are in pole position for it.

6 Dig out that old CV right now and give it a makeover. Your CV gives an impression of you and if it looks tired and old – well, what can we say? Make sure you always carry around a copy of it (even if only on a digital data stick) in case anyone asks for a copy.

7 Consider using a career coach. They can be hard taskmasters but if they help you to achieve results it could be a very useful investment in terms of time and money. (If you are being made redundant you may be entitled to see a career coach as part of that package.)

8 Consider psychometric instruments as a way to find out more about how your personality functions and therefore whether you are suited to certain industries or business areas. No one knows you better than yourself and being in the wrong industry is like trying to swim against the tide – you can do it but you are using more effort than you need. Instead find a business area that suits you and plays to your strengths.

9 You may not get everything you want. Some career areas are notoriously difficult to break into but there are other options such as working alongside them. However, don't be so focused that you forget to enjoy the journey. Life goes by too fast as it is to waste even one moment of it.

10 You have real knowledge and experience that others can benefit from. Share the good stories (and the banana skins) with others and help motivate them to see their own career success too.

Part four
Your toolkit

Activity 1 – What your career says about you

What does your career say about you?

Grab a blank piece of paper and write as a heading at the top of the paper the business you are in, and then halfway down write the job you have.

For example, you might have written:

Business: Financial Services

at the top, and then:

Credit controller

halfway down.

Under the main heading, list assumptions and perceptions people generally have about people who work in your sector (in this example, the financial services sector).

Do the same under your job title.

Put the list in a drawer for 24 hours and make a note in your diary for tomorrow to look at the list again.

The following day, retrieve the list and read it over again, adding any and questioning those assumptions and perceptions you have written – are they a fair assessment?

Now for the moment of truth. Does that list describe the person you want to be?

► If the answer is yes, then great – acknowledge that people will always see you in this way and will draw their conclusions about you from this.
► If the answer is no, then you need to be either rethinking your career choice or working to change perceptions within the career you are in.

Whatever your answer, keep reading – there is a lot more to discover yet.

Activity 2 – Through the time tunnel

Time trucks on and I want you to start thinking of time as a continuum and recognize that things happen in seasons. We learn as we travel through, and some of your early learning will help inform your career decisions later in life. You could be blocking an opportunity because of some past situation or you could be ignoring a career path that is under your very nose.

To start this activity, you will need:

▶ a long piece of clean paper (two or three smaller sheets connected together would also be fine)
▶ a pen or pencil.

On the paper draw a long horizontal line within the bottom third of the paper. Starting from the left-hand side and moving to the right, underneath the line, write the years from the age you left school through to your current age (now can you see why you need a long piece of paper?). If you have rather a long spectrum then consider numbering in twos but resist going up five years at a time because you will lose too much detail.

Now start to write above the line, over the relevant year, the jobs you have held. This should be fairly straightforward. Instantly you have a timeline of your career to date. Look at your flow of work and think about how one job led you to the next job.

In the space above that write in any influential factors that happened during those years. Not all jobs move from a smooth progression; often there are situations or events that trigger a change of thought or position. Examples of this may include:

▶ loss of a loved one, a friendship or relationship
▶ a geographical move
▶ meeting someone influential in your life
▶ taking some advice
▶ losing your job unexpectedly
▶ experiencing a change in values
▶ starting a family.

Put your time tunnel away for now and do not look at it for at least two days. You need to put some space between you and the task. Make a note in your diary as to when you will be reviewing it again.

REVIEWING YOUR TIME TUNNEL

When you take a look again at your time tunnel ask yourself these questions:

- ▶ Overall is there a pattern to my career?
- ▶ How am I making my career choices? (Am I the victim of other people's agendas or do I make my own choices?)
- ▶ If I had to run a theme through my time tunnel what would it be? Is there one aspect that connects the job roles together?
- ▶ If I had to describe my career to date in one sentence, what would it be?
- ▶ If I could design the next move, would it follow this pattern or be completely different?

Complete the time tunnel forward for the next five years – what will you write?

Activity 3 – Completing a time log

We are all so busy but where are we spending our time? You cannot try to improve your time balance until you know exactly where the time goes, and so keep a time log for about three days – you will be surprised by the results.

THE RULES!

1 Set out the three priority objectives you wish to achieve in the day. Try to express these in output or result terms, for example *not* 'meet Jan and John to discuss the project' *but* 'to secure an agreement regarding the amount of budget available on XYZ project'.
2 Begin the log as soon as you start work.
3 Log each activity and time immediately.
4 Describe each activity as precisely as possible, for example, *not* 'discussion/Jan' *but* 'budget review/Jan and John'. For speed, use abbreviations, for example, 'MG' for 'meeting'.
5 At the end of the day complete the Analysis column. This is *very important* as a start to finding improvements. For example, 'why was this done at all?', 'should have said', 'could be delegated', 'was this journey necessary?' or 'meeting badly handled'.
6 Include any evening work in your time log.

At the end of your period of completing your time log, make the following analysis:

HOURS WORKED

Add up your daily total, work out a mean average and then multiply by five for the number of hours over a full week (and then add on any weekend hours).

Actual hours worked per week	
Hours _____	Minutes _____

INTERRUPTIONS

Excluding meetings and meal breaks estimate the average time you work without some form of interruption, for example, telephone, visitor, etc.

Average time free from interruptions
Hours _____ Minutes _____

How could you work to change this to your satisfaction?

DAILY TIME LOG

Name: _____

Date: _____

Today's priorities:	Today's achievements:	Progression was made on:	Little or no progress:
1. _____	_____	_____	_____
_____	_____	_____	_____
2. _____	_____	_____	_____
_____	_____	_____	_____
3. _____	_____	_____	_____
_____	_____	_____	_____

Time of day	Activity	Time taken (mins)	Analysis (for example, Is this activity necessary? Could it be delegated?)	Did it run to time/plan? How do I feel about that?

Activity 4 – My elements of control

It is essential to be able to identify what areas are within your control.

Fold a piece of A4 paper lengthwise so that you have two columns. At the top of one write a heading: Things I can control. At the top of the other write: Things I cannot control.

Now list under each heading the things regarding your job that you either can or cannot control. For example, you may be able to control the skills you can learn, but you may not be able to control the fact that someone has to vacate that particular job before you can even apply to take their place.

1 Look at the list of things you can control and ask yourself:
   ▷ What am I doing about this?
   ▷ Am I maximizing all the opportunities here?
2 Now look at the list of things you cannot control and ask:
   ▷ I may not be able to control this but can I influence it in any way?
   ▷ Is there any other way these items (or parts of these items) can become more under my control?
3 Considering point 2 can you move any items from the 'Things I cannot control' list onto the 'Things I can control' side?
4 Look at the items you are now left with in the 'Things I cannot control' list. You need to work on a way of acceptance and self-management so that you are able to feel better about your level of input into this list.

Activity 5 – Affirmation and confirmation

Affirmations are things that sales people write to convince themselves to sell more, right? Wrong! They are helpful for everyone, and they can definitely help you.

Sometimes everyone can seem to be on a mission to knock the wind out of your sails. Believe it or not, although there are many very encouraging people in the world, there are also many who are jealous of your success or would prefer it if you did not succeed. The only person who can help you in this situation is you, but building resilience and keeping a focus on where you are going is not easy. This is where affirmation and confirmations really come into their own.

First, a bit of science. Your brain does not know whether you are lying or not. If you tell it frequently that you are a poor selfless victim, a mere pawn at the mercy of everyone else in life, it will soon start to take this seriously on board and you will find that you start to act (non-verbal communication) and phrase your sentences (verbal communication) in this way, encouraging people to react to you in this way. This then reinforces your belief – after all if everyone is treating you like this then it *must* be true.

Stop right there! That is a highway to nowhere but the logic holds that if you can programme negative things into your mind then you can also programme in positive ones. Try the following.

Let's start small. Cut out two small pieces of card, about the size of a pocket calculator. It can be from a carton (or similar) but make sure they are clear on one side so that you can write on them without any other message interfering. On one piece of card write in large clear lettering a positive statement about *yourself*. You could have any one of the following:

- ▶ You are brilliant
- ▶ You are highly intelligent
- ▶ You are strong
- ▶ Everyone loves you
- ▶ You are respected by everyone …

… or similar, whatever statement means something to you.

Now put that either in your diary, use it as a bookmark, or place it in your bedside drawer. In other words put it where you will see it several times a day but without it being obtrusive.

On the second card write a statement about what you are trying to achieve in your career, for example:

► I will have a degree by the time I am 30.
► I will own my own pottery business by the time I am 60.
► I will create enough business to become a partner by the time I am 40.

Keep this card in your pocket and look at it several times a day, every day.

The first card was an affirmation and will help with your personal confidence, and the second card is confirmation that you are on the right course for the future and will help you to focus and make the right decisions to support the future you want to create.

Finally, don't forget to revisit your affirmations and confirmations regularly. Your focus will change as you achieve and push further forward.

Activity 6 – Exercising gratitude

It is very easy to let our motivation sag when we are facing difficult situations. When you have just been told that you face possible redundancy, it is very hard to find the energy to stimulate the new, positive, creative thought necessary to put you in the right mindset for considering your alternatives.

This little exercise may seem very simple in its format but I can promise you that the results are far reaching – even on into other parts of your life. All you need are a pen or pencil, and some paper by the side of your bed.

To illustrate how this works (and so that you are ready for action later) grab a pen and paper right now and follow these three steps.

Step 1: Write down on the paper, five things that you are grateful for.

For those of you who are storming ahead on this task, go straight to step 2. The rest of you, stay with me a little longer.

If you are struggling with this task it is because you are trying to either think too deeply or you are trying to analyse the task rather than go with it. There are things we are all grateful for such as the sun rising this morning, warm socks to snuggle our toes, kind friends/supportive neighbours, a roof over our heads, the love of another person, dark winter nights that send us into a deep sleep, bright mornings that wake us up, the flowers that grow and birds that sing, the beauty of nature and the sound of music. Let your imagination run – there is no judgement being made on what you choose. This activity is not about who can think of the most rewarding gratitude but about you recognizing the beauty that is life.

Step 2: Do not qualify or try to rank any of these thoughts, just read them through a few times and let your mind acknowledge them as fact. Notice how you feel – you should feel pleasantly satisfied.

Step 3: Do this activity as the last thing you do each night before going to bed. To ease you into sleep faster, turn over the ideas in your head as you slip off. You will find you wake the following morning feeling much more positive about the day ahead and what you can achieve.

None of this activity is about denying your current situation but you cannot create a pathway forward and consider all the options open to you while you are in a negative place. By exercising gratitude you will start to think positively and creatively, and therefore see more opportunities as they arise.

Activity 7 – Meet and greet people with impact

When you meet people for the first time the initial 30 seconds are crucial. That is when they make formative assumptions about you, creating a blueprint that is very difficult to change later on. For this very reason you need to make sure that your first 30 seconds are full of impact and leave the impression you want.

Think for a moment about the last time you met a key person – perhaps you were introduced to another manager or a customer. How did you react? How prepared were you? We cannot always know that we are going to meet someone, it may be ad hoc and so we need to be sure that when we can't plan we have a confident way of meeting new people that works at a number of levels and in varying situations.

There are a number of ways of meeting and greeting people depending on how much you know them and your natural style. However, a good business failsafe is the handshake. This business greeting is useful in all situations, rarely offends and is acceptable across many cultures.

Note: Only shake someone's hand if they are introduced to you. If the situation is a little awkward and after a minute or two, no one appears to be introducing anyone, extend your hand and say, 'Let's get some introductions going, my name is...' Extend your hand and firmly shake the hand of the other person.

The perfect handshake is firm and strong without crushing the hand of the other person. Shake the other person's hand once or twice in an up-and-down motion, and then let the hand go. Practise on a friend until you can do this confidently. The limp handshake is acknowledged as one of the most off-putting business gestures, and so make sure you get this simple procedure right.

To accompany your handshake, look the other person in the eye and smile (if you feel uncomfortable with this, read through Activity 8 on reducing anxiety). Also, always have a business card to hand to ensure your introduction is not forgotten.

CREATING AN ENGAGING INTRODUCTION

When we are introduced we often also mention our job title. The problem is that job titles are rarely interesting or engaging. They do not often excite and may not even describe the fundamental aspects of your job. If you are in this situation you need to create a more dynamic introduction – a 'hook' that will create a talking point or stimulate conversation. For example, rather than saying, 'Hi, my name is John and I am a training officer here at the nursery' a more tantalizing introduction might be, 'Hi, my name is John and while the business grows plants, I grow people.'

Test out a number of introductions to your role, vary them to take in different circumstances but make sure they have impact and are engaging.

Activity 8 – Reducing anxiety

We feel anxiety when we are put in a position of stress, apprehension, worry and/or fear. That fear does not have to be real – it can be imagined, such as thinking you might fall over a cliff even though you are over three metres away from the edge.

Anxiety is identified by the heart racing, short breaths, the body breaking out into a sweat, nervous impulses being activated (such as shaking or trembling hands) and a rigidity to the body. It serves to protect us by warning us of danger and enabling us to feel fear in certain situations. It triggers the 'fight or flight' system within us, but the problem is that we no longer use this system regularly and therefore the adrenalin created to deal with it has problems dispersing.

To counter anxiety, try to regulate your breathing in three easy steps:

1 Breathe in through the nose to the count of three.
2 Hold the breath for the count of three.
3 Now exhale through the mouth to a count of three.

After doing this for a few minutes, sigh heavily and let your shoulders relax down with the out-breath. Run through this again and this time let your arms relax down as well as your shoulders (sometimes it helps to close your eyes). You will soon feel your anxiety start to subside and be overtaken by the feeling of calm.

Activity 9 – Breaking through a static mindset

Reframing problems can be a useful device for breaking through a static mindset. It is so easy to get locked into one way of thinking, or thinking that an outcome is inevitable. Do you believe in free will? That you have choice over your actions? If so, then you know that it is the way that you think and act that can change the outcome. Further, when we choose to think different things, we will gain different outcomes.

Often we are simply too close to the problem to suggest any other outcome than the one going around in our heads. This is where the blockage begins. We get locked into one way of thinking – the very way that leads to our inevitable outcome. However, if we can find a way to free the blockage all things are possible.

How do we do this? We use different words and thinking to reframe the 'problem' (note that even labelling something a 'problem' rather than a 'glitch' or 'hiccup' suddenly makes it seem so much more serious and unfixable). Let's try this with some other language:

Don't say ...	Say ...
problem	glitch, hiccup, issue
difficult	intricate, convoluted, interesting
can't	try, maybe, possibly
impossible	puzzling, tricky, experimental

If your mindset says, 'I can't move on from this job, I have no skills' every time you repeat this to yourself, you are building that wall higher by confirming this as the truth.

Instead try saying, 'I want to move on from this job and I am working towards the skills necessary.' Suddenly there is action and intent and the mindset is broken, letting loose a whole range of future possibilities.

The next time you feel that there is nothing to be done about a problem, start by rewording the problem. This will crack through the static mindset and open up the possibilities.

Identify one mindset block that is getting in the way of you expanding further in your career. Write it down and then write the sentence again, reframing the words. For example:

'I don't see the point in this, there is no answer to this problem.'

(Reframed) 'These are interesting issues and it seems that the key to this is lost and we need to find it.'

Notice how the first sentence leaves you with nowhere to go, while the other suggests a playful activity.

Now try to incorporate this technique into your career thoughts, even if only to yourself, and notice what happens. You may find you now generate a whole new range of ideas.

Activity 10 – One nice thing

There are two aspects of looking good. The first is how we present ourselves, our clothes, our style and so forth. All things we can enhance and do our best with, but it is up to the beholder as to whether they find that acceptable. In other words this is an external aspect of looking good (and one that can be sorted out by a stylist or an honest friend!).

The second aspect of looking good is how you *feel* you look. We all have ideas in our heads of how we think we look, and although it may bear no resemblance to reality it has a huge effect on our self-esteem and the way we present ourselves. We can dress head to toe in designer gear but if we feel we look like a fashion victim then no amount of expensive clothing will help that. You only have to look at how anyone attractive can be wracked by fear that their hair does not look nice.

Here we go – grab a piece of paper and a pen and write down on one side of it all the things you like about yourself. Don't stop until you have exhausted the list.

Now turn the paper over and write down a list of all the things you don't like about yourself.

I don't usually bet but were I to do so I would put my money on the list of things you don't like about yourself being longer than the list of things you do like. Unfortunately we can find fault with ourselves so much more easily than we can praise our good points.

This has to change now! If you are going to go forward in your career you need to have confidence in your appearance. This can be a very long journey for many people but every journey starts with a first step – and this is your first step.

Take an honest look at yourself in the mirror. What features do you like about yourself? At this stage ignore anything else. Perhaps you have put on a few pounds but you have lovely eyes, or a graceful neck. Do you have trim ankles or nicely proportioned hands? Unusual colouring or smooth skin? The list can be as long as you like – don't hold back, but equally you can do this exercise if you only identify 'one nice thing'.

Whatever you have decided, these are the areas you are now going to acknowledge to yourself and adorn as appropriate. What do I mean by that? Every day you are going to say to yourself (or in the mirror), 'Of course you have such pretty ankles/delicate skin (or whatever)' and admire them. Also when you next go to buy clothes, make-up, jewellery or whatever adornment you choose, you must bear this in mind. For example, if you have trim ankles then ask the assistant to select a skirt length, or shoe style that shows them to their best advantage. If you have strong hands that you want to emphasize, consider the right jewellery or watch that brings attention to them. In other words, choose your best features and:

▶ acknowledge them to yourself daily
▶ ensure that they are the features noticed by others.

You will find that by doing this your self-confidence will increase immeasurably and you will also start to rethink your grooming so that you show aspects of yourself to their best advantage.

Activity 11 – Your skills

Grab a pen and a piece of paper and think about all the compliments you have received for your work over the years. Each time you think of something, write it down. Start at school age and carry on through education – perhaps you were told at school that you were known for the quality of your work or that you had good analysis skills. Extend that forward into the jobs that you have had – what compliments have you received, where have you excelled?

Don't limit this exercise to work; think about the comments of family and friends – there is no need to be over modest as no one is going to see this except you. Write down as many compliments as you can remember.

When you have exhausted your comments, using the diagram in this activity, place your skills in the various circles. You will notice that there are areas where the circles overlap and that some skills fall in these areas. You may even have skills that feature in the centre area where all three merge.

This activity will help you to see where your skills lie.

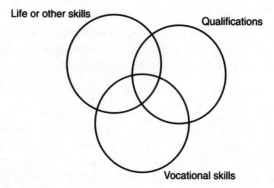

Figure 11.1 Skills Venn diagram.

Activity 12 – Creating an action plan

Action plans are a great way of structuring a project, and that project can be a work project or something you want to achieve for yourself. Action plans are essentially a tool for getting things done and moving projects forward. Emphasis is on the word 'Action' and this means 'doing an activity'. (You cannot put anything in the plan that you cannot in some way control.)

To start with you need to know what you want to achieve and that may be in the form of a statement or some objectives. If the statement is very large, for example, 'to move into the grade above by next year' it needs to be broken down into smaller steps, such as:

► Research senior grade through the job description
► Skills-map the job description requirement against my current skills ...

... and so forth. It will make the process more manageable and you will be able to chart your progress.

As a rule of thumb, break down any action that would take you longer than an hour as it is unlikely you will achieve it unless you have hours to devote to this work.

Grade each action against their level of importance using a sliding scale. If an action is very important to the overall outcome give it a '1'; if is it not very important at all mark it as '10'.

Now look at all the number '1' items and decide on what order you will achieve them, then move to the '2' items and so forth.

Book time in your diary or planner to achieve the first item (note that as you start to achieve items others move up into their place and become the next most important item. Your action plan is never static; it is a moving document that charts your progress. The plans are made to be rewritten. Nothing is cast in stone and therefore plan to refocus, change course and adjust your plan based on your continued thoughts and experience.

If you find that you cannot achieve a given task in the required amount of time, then it needs breaking down further or rolling forward into your next plan.

You can have action plans that run over a year, or a month, longer-term ones that chart the key stages for the next five years, or one that gets you through the following week. There are no hard-and-fast rules.

Activity 13 – Who do I think I am?

We all have a different view of ourselves than that of others, but it is who *you* think you are that is important – not fitting a mould that other people are trying to push you into. But how much do you know yourself? Have you ever thought about what you really excel at and what you like doing? They are not always the same thing.

For this activity you need a sheet of A4 paper and a pen or pencil. Fold the paper down the middle lengthways so that you have two columns, and then open it again. Put a heading at the top of one side that says: Things I liked. At the top of the second column put: Things I did not like.

Down the paper on both sides put the names of your previous employers. For example:

Things I liked	Things I did not like
Johnson's Bakery	Johnson's Bakery
Quest Insurance	Quest Insurance
Mace Supermarket	Mace Supermarket

Now fold one half behind the other so that you can only see one column in front of you. This will stop you being distracted.

Write under each employer a list of the things you liked about working there. When you have come to a natural finish, turn the paper over and repeat the exercise on the other side – things you did not like. It will look something like the example below.

When you have finished, open out the sheet of paper. Look at the details in the two columns. Take away the headings from each job or copy the words out without the job titles. You are now left with a list of things you enjoyed in employment (and therefore you need to ensure some of these are built into any future employment) and a list of things that are real no-go areas for you (areas you need to stay away from).

Things I liked	Things I did not like
Johnson's Bakery	Johnson's Bakery
flexibility	getting dirty
the hours	early starts
friends	
Quest Insurance	Quest Insurance
the people	paperwork
working part time	meetings
	having to deliver on time
Mace Supermarket	Mace Supermarket
chatting to customers	wearing a uniform
working part time	having to work at the
cheaper food	weekend
	having a supervisor who
	watched you

Put the page in a drawer for a couple of days before looking at it again. Check that you have the main points in place, and then use these as your criteria for any future employment choices.

Activity 14 – Keeping a motivation diary

What motivates you? We are all motivated by different things and what might motivate one person will not motivate the next.

Motivation is not the same as feeling happy. To feel motivated is to feel the energy to do something, it is a 'need' rather than a 'want' and can be within us at a very deep, subliminal level. When people are motivated to succeed they might not have the conscious thought 'I must succeed' 20 times a day, but they find that behind every decision they make an unconscious desire focuses their thinking and leads the decision for them. For example, you might not have the conscious desire to attend a dinner that your influential boss is attending – you really might not want to go at all, but when asked you find yourself saying 'yes' immediately because you know subliminally that you must be there.

Try to keep a motivation diary for one week so that you can see where your drivers are. It is quite easy to make one: label a blank sheet of paper with the day of the week at the top. Down the left-hand side put the times of the day in ten-minute blocks. Across the top of the sheet have two columns, labelled 'Action' and 'Motivation'. It should look a little like this:

Monday 12 February

Time	Action	My motivation
8.00	ate breakfast	I am hungry
8.10	dashed upstairs	alarm went off
8.20	left house	got to get to work

In this example we can see that a lot of the actions are regular ones that are more like habitual patterns than true motivators – but if we stick with this throughout the day we start to find ...

Time	Action	My motivation
14.00	cleared filing	I need to control
14.10	cleaned filing area	need this area to be clear
14.20	ate chocolate biscuit	reward for clearing filing

This type of motivation starts to show a need for neatness and a feeling of control over the office. The motivators and actions start to show us what drives this person and where their motivation lies. Like all things in life this knowledge can be used to good or bad effect.

Activity 15 – Image checklist

Before you begin, have a firm image in your mind of the style you want to emulate.

Make sure it is a style that is worn by those in the career you want and at the level you want.

I have thought through which colours are the most acceptable at work	
I have considered that I might need work clothes that perform functions, for example, have lots of pockets	
If there is a 'dress-down' day I have considered how acceptable this is for everyone and whether I should join in	
I have identified which of my daytime wear is the best-quality item I have	
I have identified which of my working wear fits best	
I have identified which of my shoes are the best presented	
I have decided which shoes need to be repaired	
I have checked that I have a good coat that fits well	
I have thought about which accessories are acceptable at work	
I have studied which of my accessories show flair	
I have considered my hairstyle for ease of grooming and maintenance	
I have thought through an effective personal grooming regime that enables me to get to work on time	
I have adjusted my workstation or workplace to suit my height and ease any muscle strain	
I am starting to be more aware of how I move around the workplace, and understand that I may be judged on this	
I am starting to think through how I work with others and consider them in the workplace	

Activity 16 – Future predictions

I cannot know the future for all the occupations of everyone reading this book, and therefore for this activity I need a bit of help from the person mostly likely to know this information – you! Therefore we are going to dig around in your subconscious to find it.

This is what futurologists do when trying to dream or anticipate the future, and you can do it too.

1 Find yourself a comfortable spot where you can daydream freely without being interrupted.

2 Make sure you have a pen and paper by your side.

3 Close your eyes and start to see yourself in your dream job. What are you doing? How are you acting? Who is around you? What does your workplace look like?

4 When you feel comfortable with that image, project yourself forward five years. Now what are you doing? Are there computers? People? Do you have an assistant? Are you in a workplace? Working from home? Abroad?

5 When you feel comfortable with what you 'see' make a quick note on the pad of the things you will need to know to live this life. For example, if you have an assistant then you must need to know how to manage people. If everything is computerized, do you need help with that?

6 Review what you have written and give each of them a mark out of ten for how realistic you think they might be. Don't be too censorious – if you have wacky ideas that's just fine.

7 Ask yourself how this list transfers into skills that you need to attain so that you are in the position of being ready for such a future.

Activity 17 – Perk me ups!

Make a list here of all the good things your current job offers.
If you can't think of them all at once put the list aside for another
day. Think of everything from free drinks to air conditioning,
and then reflect on how it would feel to lose these. (You could
always use this list in the future to see whether it adds up to a
better package from another company – or just keep it for future
negotiating.

Activity 18 – Goal setting for winners

If you feel you have seen activities on goal setting before, you are in danger of skipping over this page and in doing so missing a real trick. If that is you …

STOP RIGHT THERE!

… and reconsider.

Goals are not just something that you put in place to please the company at appraisal time – they are a living, breathing part of every day. Every time you draw up a 'to do' list or make an itinerary of what you are going to do this weekend you are setting goals.

Setting goals makes things happen. I am not going to apologize for saying that again – setting goals makes things happen. People who don't set goals have no guidelines to what they should be doing with their time or with their life, or know when they have achieved anything.

'I need to sell ten of these a day just to keep my job' focuses the mind in the way that 'I need to sell these' never will. In this situation the first person will be very focused on their achievement whereas the second person may feel the issue is on their agenda, but not critical, and if another 'important' issue pops up – then there is always tomorrow. To make ourselves perform we sometimes have to set goals with tough boundaries, otherwise other people simply get there first.

Drawing up good-quality goals is crucial to success. You need them to be SMART – and that means:

S – specific

M – measurable

A – achievable

R – realistic

T – time-based.

For example: To update my CV with my recent projects by 4.30 this afternoon.

This is short and to the point, and would now make you focus on completing that task – possibly something you had been putting off until you had more time or a gap in your day (which of course never happens).

Start to view goal setting not as yet another task in your day, but a way of helping you to structure a plan for your day – a plan in which you include a couple of stretching goals to take your career forward.

Activity 19 – Networking essentials

I am sure you have at some time asked someone how they came to find that job or project (which you did not see advertised) and they reply that 'someone I know told me about it'. Yes, it's frustrating but this is why having a strong network is hugely important – this is how dynamic people move from position to position and find unique opportunities that just don't appear anywhere else. The wonderful thing about a network is that it carries on from where you are. In other words, you know people who then know others, who also know other people, and so the network opens out in a myriad of opportunities.

At this point you may be thinking, 'I want one of these' but the truth is that you probably already have a network but you just don't think of it as such.

Start by grabbing a plain piece of paper and put your name in the middle of it. Draw some lines coming out of your name like rays of sun, and put a name of someone you know on each. The names can be family, friends, neighbours, colleagues – it doesn't matter as long as you know them.

Now choose one name and think who they have introduced you to or someone else they know. Move onto the next name and so forth. Don't worry if you cannot identify anyone from one name, just move onto the next.

You will now be creating a rich picture of interlocking names, some of which may be known by two or three people. If there are links to others, then use a dotted line to show that link.

It is important that you carry on with this (and it might take you some time) until you have a full picture or graphic representation of your network. Suddenly, instead of having two or three people you might ask about a future job in (say) journalism, you may have over 100 when you use the network.

When you have your network in place (note you will continue to add to it as you meet more and more people) think through the best way for you to interact with everyone. You could send personal messages, create a social networking site, send regular 'hello' cards or celebration cards, hold a networking party –

anything! But whatever you do keep your network going and keep adding to it.

It is great to be able to see a pictorial representation of your network but how do you interact with all these people? How can you push a message out to them all and use them to find a new job? The answer to this lies in signing up to a professional networking site such as LinkedIn. It is free to sign up and, after searching for your colleagues (and linking to them), the power of the mighty search engine then trawls through people with a similar profile to yours and suggests links. If there is a particular company you would like to work for try finding the key person you need to speak to and search for them. It just might be that they have a presence on such a site and you could make contact with them that way.

Activity 20 – Visualization

Sports professionals and athletes use visualization as a technique to help them not only to focus but also predetermine their outcome. To give you an example of how visualization can work (albeit negatively), imagine that you have a presentation coming up. Now close your eyes and see yourself walking into that room. Your clothes don't feel right and you tell yourself that you should not have worn that particular outfit. In thinking about this you fail to see that the carpet is rucked and you stumble over it, dropping your notes in the process. Everyone is staring at you as you collect your material and your face has gone red. Stop for a moment and visualize how you feel at that moment. Imagine that you had done this just prior to a real presentation – do you think that you would now feel confident and give the best presentation ever? No, because you have visualized the worse and in preparation for this adrenalin is coursing through your body and this alone will make you jumpy and excitable. After the presentation you may even slump into a mild depression, negating any benefit from the experience at all.

I am sure that as you went through that activity you could see how the negative visualization worked against you. Now that you have seen the power of this activity, you need to use it to enhance your performance. Close your eyes again but this time imagine yourself to be tall and confident. You feel good in your clothes and you stride out towards the presenting table. Your very presence stills the active audience and they await your findings with pens raised, ready to take down the nuggets of information as you start to talk. They are so engaged with the presentation that they are carried through to the end on a wave of interest, and you end to the sound of thunderous applause. Back in the real world, if you now had to step out and provide a presentation would that visualization increase your confidence?

The wonderful thing about a visualization is that no one needs to know that you are doing it. Start now, creating top-level visualizations that you can use in any aspect of your career. The richer you make your visualizations the more effective they will be, so consider:

▶ Vision – What does the place look like? What colours surround you? Look in your virtual mirror at yourself – what do you see? A businessperson? A professional?

- ► Sounds – What sounds can you hear? Are there sounds in the background?
- ► Smell – Are you wearing any perfume or aftershave? If so, what does it smell like? Does the room smell?
- ► Touch – What does the paper feel like in your hand? How does the desk feel under your papers, or the chair you are sitting on?
- ► Bodily awareness – How are you feeling? How does your body feel from the inside?

Visualize yourself in a totally new career area and visualize your performance – the results might surprise you.

Activity 21 – Dealing with stress

Stress is more than feeling pressured. We all need a certain amount of tension and pressure in our lives otherwise we would never achieve anything let alone get up in the morning! However, searching for a new job can be very stressful, especially if you keep meeting blocks to your progression or you are not happy in your current situation. Suddenly you feel an enormous strain to simply keep going, and that feeling can manifest itself as physical symptoms such as shortness of breath, racing pulse and anxiety attacks.

If you think you may be heading in this direction the first course of action is to keep a stress diary. This is simply a diary in which you note down when you feel stressed and what you think the cause is. This will show you patterns of behaviour such as whether you feel worse at certain times in the day. It will also reveal to you what might be the cause. For example, you may have thought that your work is the cause, but it might be that you are trying to do too much at the weekends.

When you feel stressed, try some of the following:

- ▶ Take a break – We all need to refresh our batteries from time to time. Sometimes just an hour spent doing something else is all that is needed.
- ▶ Massage – Indulge in time spent on you, whether that be a massage or any other treatment that allows you to be relaxed and have a little 'me' time.
- ▶ Yoga and exercise – To reduce stress you can either slow the body down or rev it up, the choice is yours.
- ▶ Talking therapies – Psychotherapy and counselling can be very helpful in enabling you to express your feelings in a safe environment.
- ▶ Books and CDs – Some people find that reading a book that takes you to another world, or listening to music (or alternatively a soothing recording) is very relaxing.
- ▶ Self-hypnosis – This is a technique anyone can learn to enable them to relax at will in any situation.
- ▶ Health and nutrition – You need a well body to fight stress. Check your diet to ensure you are getting all the nutrients you need.

Note: if stress continues, you must see your doctor or physician.

Activity 22 – The elevator speech

This is a short, 15- to 30-second sound bite that introduces you succinctly and memorably to a potential customer or contact. Elevator speeches should be memorized so they can be delivered effortlessly and without any hint of mumbling. They are for the chance encounters in life when you might meet useful contacts briefly and want to introduce yourself in an impressive way that might result in a further conversation.

PREPARE YOUR ELEVATOR SPEECH – AS EASY AS 1, 2, 3

1 Firstly, you need to think in terms of the benefits you are offering. People are always fascinated by things that improve their lives or better their existence. Saying, 'Hi, my name is Ben and I am in recruiting' is boring but saying, 'Hi, my name is Ben and I partner companies that need talented people to help build excellence' is far more impressive, and now you have my full attention!

2 Now follow that up by giving an example: 'Hi, my name is Ben and I partner companies that need talented people to help build excellence. I recently helped a business increase its profits by over 50 per cent through three simple actions' – this gives credibility.

3 Lastly build in a call to action: 'Hi, my name is Ben and I partner companies that need talented people to help build excellence. I recently helped a business increase its profits by over 50 per cent through three simple actions. If you would like to find out how I did that, here's my card. I think you would be fascinated.'

Who could resist that?

Activity 23 – Assessing values

What do you value in your working life? Here are some examples:

- ▶ Money?
- ▶ Friendship?
- ▶ Working in a close team?
- ▶ Being very independent?
- ▶ Working for an 'ethical' organization?
- ▶ Having lots of work opportunities?
- ▶ A job for life?
- ▶ Being able to take risks?
- ▶ Knowing that you are helping others?
- ▶ Being close to the customer?
- ▶ Working outside?
- ▶ Creating things of beauty?
- ▶ Being able to make decisions?
- ▶ Organizing your own workload?
- ▶ Seeing projects through to the end?
- ▶ Getting new ideas up and running?

These will give you an idea but there are so many others. Make a list of the top ten principles that you value in your workplace and workspace. (They don't necessarily have to be from this list.)

Now condense that list down to your top three – the values that you would find it very difficult to compromise on.

These are the values you need to have reflected in your work for you to feel contented. If we work against our value system we feel stressed and personally compromised. For example, if you value social interaction and end up working alone, or if you value working for society and end up in a capitalist organization that is only interested in profit you will feel severely out of step at work and this will create tension and unhappiness.

Activity 24 – Creating a killer CV

Locate your CV and check the contents. Firstly, is it up to date? If not, don't worry – in ten minutes you can brush up your CV and be ready to move your career forward.

Now, look at the format and ask yourself:

- ▶ Does it look professional?
- ▶ Is it well spaced out (columns of information evenly presented and so forth)?
- ▶ Is it no longer than two pages?
- ▶ Is the information provided in a clear, professional font – nothing fancy?

If any of these factors are missing, read on …

When you create a CV you need to be very clear about what you want the CV to be. Is it:

- ▶ For handing out whenever an opportunity arises? In this case your CV is likely to be fairly general but showcasing your experience and best attributes.
- ▶ For sending out to specific organizations? In this case your CV needs to be very focused, showcasing skills that you know are key to that particular industry.
- ▶ For sending in answer to a job application? Your CV must be very focused on the job description and must answer as many questions as possible, showing your suitability in every area mentioned …

… and you may have other reasons. In fact you may have several reasons, in which case it can help to have several CVs. The biggest sin is not to have an up-to-date CV languishing on your computer at all. You never know when someone will ask for one.

Layout – Keep it simple. Start off with personal details: name address, contact details and NI number and/or driving ability. Then list the qualifications you have, in reverse order (with your most recent qualifications first).

Previous employers – Next is your list of previous employers. This is to demonstrate your experience but there is more than one way of displaying this information, and depends on how you want to present your facts.

Deciding on format – There are two main ways you can lay out your previous experience. Choose the style that fits your situation.

Chronological	Functional
You are continuing in the same function or industry	You are making a significant career or job change
Your career shows steady growth and development with progressive responsibilities	You want to emphasize skills and competencies not used in recent work experience
Your job objective is similar to recent experience	Your job objective is different from your experience
Previous employers have been prominent/prestigious	Your experience is gained in different, relatively unconnected jobs
You are applying for a position in a highly traditional field or organization	You have been employed by the same company for a very long time
You have an unbroken employment record/no gaps	You have a history of frequent job changes or gaps in employment or you are entering the job market after an absence
A chronological format calls the reader's attention to your recent job history and experience	A functional format directs the reader's attention to your functional strengths

Hobbies – I personally do not like to see a list of hobbies as they do not often add much to the strength of the CV (after all you are there to sell your *work* skills). Also most people are short of space on CVs in which case they will not have lines to spare. On the other hand, hobbies do show a well-rounded person and can possibly be an ice-breaker in interviews.

Length – While we are talking about length, try to stick within the two-page rule. HR managers particularly will not have time to read more than this about each candidate.

Using 'keywords' – Finally, grab attention by using key words. CVs are often sorted through a computerized filtering system. The operator will put in key words they are looking for such as 'negotiating' or 'team management' and the filter system will collate the relevant CVs for greater scrutiny. Also be very precise with your terminology: 'contributing to a team' is very different from 'managing a team' – make sure you use the right word and are able to justify it. Mirror the words used either verbally by the manager or on the job description.

Activity 25 – Creating a personal profile

Personal profiles provide an opportunity to let the reader see the real you. They can be quite similar to a press release and should:

- ▶ never be more than one page in length
- ▶ be written in the third person
- ▶ contain a photo (if you would like to)
- ▶ provide the highlights
- ▶ be a personal sales document.

First of all, decide on the focus of the personal profile, and what you are selling. For example, if I want to tell people the extent of my experience then I will want to include examples of my experience, whereas if I want to tell people about my private life I would want to include information about my family. Once you have the focus, write a list of statements you want to include.

Look at your list of statements and see whether any could be grouped. For example, were I to have created a new database for a hospital on two occasions in my career, I would not write:

'In 1994, Karen created a database for ...', and then later 'In 2002, Karen created another database ...' – that is so boring! Instead, I would write 'Karen has worked extensively in computing and has produced databases for two major hospitals.' Notice how we skim along the top of the story and have not skimped on using dramatic words such as 'extensively' and 'major'.

It can seem strange to write about yourself in this way at first, but you will find that you become used to it, in time.

Taking it further

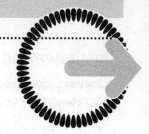

Taking it further

Avery, M. *Be Your Own Boss*, 2010, Hodder Education

Bolles, R. N. *What Colour is Your Parachute?*, 2010, Ten Speed Press

Buckingham, M. *Go Put Your Strengths to Work*, 2008, Simon & Schuster

Buzan, T. *The Mind Map Book*, 2009, BBC Active

Coombs, F. *Motivate Yourself and Reach Your Goals*, 2010, Teach Yourself

Franks L. *The SEED Handbook*, 2005, Hay House

Gray, J. *Get That Job With The Right CV*, 2010, Hodder Education

Harrington, B. *Career Management & Work/Life Integration*, 2007, Sage

Hill, L. A. *Becoming a Manager*, 2003, Harvard Business School Press

Hinds, R. & Kay, D. *A Practical Guide to Mentoring*, 2009, How to Books

Houghton, A. *Finding Square Holes: Discover Who You Really Are and Find the Perfect Career*, 2005, Crown House Publishing

Megginson, D. *Continuing Professional Development*, 2007, Chartered Institute of Personnel Management

Mayo, S. *I Can't Believe I Get Paid To Do This*, 2004, Gold Leaf Publishing

Vickers, A. & Bavister, S. *Present Yourself with Impact and Confidence*, 2010, Hodder Education

Institutes and business studies

Chartered Management Institute,
Management House, Cottingham Road, Corby, Northants,
NN17 1TT, 01536 204222 – www.managers.org.uk

Chartered Institute of Personnel Development,
151 The Broadway, London, SW19 1JQ, 020 86126200 –
www.cipd.co.uk

Chartered Institute of Marketing,
Moor Hall, Cookham, Maidenhead, Berks, SL6 9QH,
01628 427120 – www.cim.co.uk

Institute of Administrative Management,
6 Graphite Square, Vauxhall Walk, London, SE11 5EE,
020 7091 2600 – www.instam.org

Institute for the Management of Information Systems,
5 Kingfisher House, New Mill Road, Orpington, Kent, BR5 3QG,
0700 00 23456 – www.imis.org.uk

Institute of Sales and Marketing Management,
Harrier Court, Lower Woodside, Bedfordshire, LU1 4DQ,
01582 840001 – www.ismm.co.uk

Chamber of Commerce – see your local Yellow Pages

Department for Business, Innovation and Skills (BIS),
020 7215 5000 – www.bis.gov.uk

Training

Local colleges – see your local Yellow Pages

Adult Education Courses – contact your local Council

NVQs – www.direct.gov.uk

Careers advice (Next Step initiative)– www.nextstep.direct.gov.uk

Training (open learning)

The Open University, PO Box 71, Milton Keynes, MK1 6AG, 0845 300 6090 – www.open.ac.uk

Networking

Women's Business Forum, 0845 604 8183 – www.thewomensbusinessforum.co.uk

European Women's Management Development International Network – www.ewmd.org

LinkedIn – www.linkedin.com

Notes

Notes

Notes

Notes

Notes

Notes

Notes

Notes

Index

Image credits